Tina Fey

TV Comedy Superstar

Michael A. Schuman

Enslow Publishers, Inc.
40 Industrial Road
Box 398
Berkeley Heights, NJ 07922
USA
http://www.enslow.com

To Trisha and Allie, my own comedians

Library of Congress Cataloging-in-Publication Data

Schuman, Michael A.
  Tina Fey : TV comedy superstar / Michael A. Schuman.
    p. cm. — (People to know today)
  Summary: "A biography of comedy writer and actress Tina Fey"—Provided by publisher.
  Includes bibliographical references and index.
  ISBN 978-0-7660-3557-7
  1. Fey, Tina, 1970- Juvenile literature. 2. Television actors and actresses—United States—
Biography—Juvenile literature. 3. Women television writers—United States—Biography—
Juvenile literature. 4. Women comedians—United States--Biography—Juvenile literature.
5. Women television producers and directors—United States—Biography—Juvenile literature.
I. Title.
  PN2287.F4255S38 2010
  791.4502'8092—dc22
  [B]
                        2010010276

Printed in the United States of America

122010 Lake Book Manufacturing, Inc., Melrose Park, IL

10 9 8 7 6 5 4 3 2 1

To Our Readers: This book has not been authorized by Tina Fey.

We have done our best to make sure all Internet addresses in this book were active and appropriate
when we went to press. However, the author and publisher have no control over and assume no
liability for the material available on those Internet sites or on other Web sites they may link to.
Any comments or suggestions can be sent by e-mail to comments@enslow.com or to the address
on the back cover.

♻ Enslow Publishers, Inc., is committed to printing our books on recycled paper. The paper in
every book contains 10% to 30% post-consumer waste (PCW). The cover board on the outside
of each book contains 100% PCW. Our goal is to do our part to help young people and the
environment too!

Photos and Illustrations: Associated Press, pp. 1, 4, 28, 41, 52, 66, 71, 79, 82, 96; Chris
Haston/© NBC/Courtesy: Everett Collection, p. 80; Courtesy: Everett Collection, pp. 17, 34, 37;
Dana Edelson / © NBC / Courtesy: Everett Collection, pp. 88, 93; Mitchell Haaseth/© NBC/
Courtesy: Everett Collection, p. 7; © NBC/Courtesy: Everett Collection, p. 15; © Paramount/
courtesy Everett Collection, pp. 56, 58; © Universal/courtesy Everett Collection, p. 74.

Cover Illustrations: Associated Press (Tina Fey from the shoulders up).

CONTENTS

PEOPLE to KNOW TODAY

Tina Fey

1

30 ROCK ROCKS!

No one could accuse Tina Fey of taking things easy. For nine years, she was both a writer and actor on the classic television show, *Saturday Night Live*. She then wrote the script for and acted in the movie *Mean Girls*, a smash hit in 2004. Now in 2006, she was going to tackle something even bigger and more pressure filled. She was about to write and act in her own regular television comedy series.

She based her new show on her years at *Saturday Night Live*. It was titled *30 Rock*, the nickname for NBC's street address in New York City: 30 Rockefeller Plaza.

Fey had to devote full time to *30 Rock*. Acting in a regular television show meant she was at the studio five days a week. She was also working on scripts seven days a week.

Every weekday in the summer of 2006, Fey left her apartment at about six o'clock in the morning. She did not return home until about nine o'clock at night. At first, she rarely saw her baby daughter, Alice. It was then arranged that she could bring Alice to the studio when convenient.

Those who work on new television are almost always concerned that their shows will flop. In fact, most new television programs last less than a year.

But Fey had a positive attitude and a backup plan. She said that if *30 Rock* failed, she would at least be able to spend more time with Alice. Her hectic schedule made her appreciate working mothers. That was especially true one time when Alice had a bad cold. Fey spent fifteen hours a day working on *30 Rock*. Then she was awake much of the night taking care of her sick baby. That caused Fey to say to all working people, "That lady next to you at your day job probably got thrown up on last night."[1]

Fey soon discovered she had to deal with a unique problem. Another series based on *Saturday Night Live* would also be airing in the fall of 2006—*Studio 60 on the Sunset Strip*. Its chief writer was the highly talented and respected scriptwriter Aaron Sorkin. Many experts felt anything Sorkin wrote would be hard to top. Fey said, "It's just bad luck for me that in my first attempt at prime time [television] I'm going up against the most powerful writer on television."[2]

Tina Fey and Alec Baldwin as Liz and Jack on the first season of *30 Rock*.

Unlike *30 Rock, Studio 60 on the Sunset Strip* was a drama. Unlike *30 Rock,* it was an hour long. Both programs were to air on the same network, NBC. Some critics said there would not be enough people interested in watching two fictional television programs about life behind the scenes at a real television program.

Fey's *30 Rock* costar Alec Baldwin announced, "I'd be stunned if NBC picked up both shows. And ours has the tougher task, as a comedy, because if it is not funny, that's it. Whereas a drama can start off as a hard-hitting medical show about real issues, and before you count to three, it's about who's [dating] who."[3]

30 Rock had problems soon after its debut show. There are so many characters that *30 Rock* had trouble finding a focus. Viewers generally did not find the first few episodes funny. But within a few weeks, Fey and her staff discovered that the relationship between her character Liz and Liz's boss Jack, played by Baldwin, was becoming the show's main focus. Fey explained that "somewhere around the fifth or sixth episode, we started to realize that [the Liz-Jack] dynamic was really working for us."[4]

The majority of television critics agreed and *30 Rock* started to receive rave reviews. But it did not have huge numbers of viewers. Although *30 Rock's* audience was small compared to other comedies, it consisted of the more educated and wealthiest viewers. Commercial television is paid for by advertising from sponsors.

30 Rock's audience were among the most likely to spend money on products and services advertised during the show.

So despite its low numbers of viewers, on April 4, 2007, *30 Rock* was renewed for a second season.

In September 2007, *30 Rock* was awarded a great honor for any television program. It won the Emmy award for "outstanding comedy series." Emmy awards are given by the National Academy of Television Arts and Sciences. Fey mocked her show's low audience numbers when she accepted the award on national television. She publicly thanked *30 Rock*'s "dozens and dozens of viewers."[5]

30 Rock's main competition, *Studio 60 on the Sunset Strip*, was canceled after its first season.

2
SITTING WITH THE
BRAINIAC NERDS

Tina Fey's real name is Elizabeth Stamatina Fey. Her middle name reflects her Greek heritage. Her Greek-American mother's real name was Zenovia Xenakes until she married Tina's father, Donald Fey. Since Zenovia is awkward to pronounce, Tina's mother's friends called her Jeanne. Her father is of German and Scottish descent. Tina was born on May 18, 1970, in Upper Darby, Pennsylvania, outside Philadelphia. She has a brother named Peter who is eight years older than she.

Neither of Tina's parents were in show business. Her mother worked for a broker, a person who finds ways to help people best invest their money. Her father was a grant proposal writer for the University of Pennsylvania. As a grant writer, he wrote letters to people to try to get them to donate money to the university.

Despite the fact that neither of Tina's parents had jobs relating to comedy, they both were funny people who loved to laugh. Unlike many parents, Jeanne and Donald had no problem with their children watching television. They often watched television with them. They allowed them to watch comedies as long as they considered them quality programs.

One popular cartoon of the 1960s was a half-hour-long comedy titled *The Flintstones*. It was created by television cartoon producers Joseph Barbera and William Hanna. The animated show was planned to appeal to adults as well as children. *The Flintstones* was the first cartoon televised in the evening, what is known as prime time.[1]

The Flintstones was inspired by a live-action comedy titled *The Honeymooners* that originally aired in the 1950s. *The Honeymooners* was a situation comedy, or sitcom. A sitcom features the same cast of characters in the same setting every week. *The Honeymooners* starred comedians Jackie Gleason and Art Carney as buddies who constantly argued with each other but were best friends underneath. Gleason's character was a grumpy but loving man and Carney was his naïve neighbor. Audrey Meadows and Jane Keen played their understanding wives.

Barbera and Hanna decided to set their show in the Stone Age. The main characters were named Fred and Wilma Flintstone. Their best friends were Barney and Betty Rubble. The Flintstones and the Rubbles lived like suburban couples but in a Stone Age setting. Barbera admitted he hired a former writer for *The Honeymooners* to write some scripts for *The Flintstones.*[2]

The Flintstones was an immediate hit. In the 1960-1961 television season it was the eighteenth most watched television show.[3] During the next two seasons, it finished in the top thirty most-watched shows.[4] It seemed that television audiences loved *The Flintstones.*

That is, with one exception: the Fey family. Tina said, "We're all comedy fans in my family. My parents mainly wouldn't let me watch stuff that was either annoying to them, or just garbage. My dad wouldn't let us watch *The Flintstones* if he was home, because he said it was a rip-off of *The Honeymooners.* So there was some discerning taste. And we certainly did other stuff, but yeah, we watched a lot of TV."[5]

When Tina was about five, she experienced an event that seemed to have come directly from a dramatic script. Tina was in front of her home when she was attacked by someone with a knife. Fey does not like to discuss the incident.[6] However, her husband Jeff Richmond said, "It was in, like, the front yard of her house, and someone who just came up [and attacked her], and she just thought someone marked her with a pen."[7] The attack left a scar on her face.

Although Fey rarely discusses the attack, she once did answer a reporter who asked if she felt less attractive because of the scar. She answered, "I don't think so. Because I proceeded unaware of it. I was a very confident little kid."[8]

About the same time, *Saturday Night Live*, known as *SNL* for short, premiered. Decades later, it still airs live from New York City at 11:30 on Saturday night.

SNL was like no other television program before it. For ages, Saturday night at 11:30 was a time when television audiences were small. Young people were out at parties or on dates. Older people were already asleep. Figuring few people were watching television at that time, programmers filled it with reruns and old movies. But *Saturday Night Live* gave people, especially those in their teens and twenties, a reason to stay home.

SNL dripped with satire, some of it outrageous. Sketches openly mocked the president and other politicians. *SNL* also lampooned everything from the toy industry to organized religion. Some sketches, such as the recurring samurai deli—a deli counter worker who cut meat with a samurai sword—were plainly offbeat and weird. To this day, every episode has a different guest host. It is often a person from the world of show business. However, guest hosts have included athletes, newscasters, and politicians. Backing up the guest host is a regular cast of professional comedians.

At just five, Tina was too young to stay up to watch *SNL*. This was long before DVRs existed, and videotape recorders were just becoming popular. Her brother, Peter, came to the rescue. At thirteen years old, he could stay up late on Saturdays. On Sunday morning, he would act out the skits from the previous night's show for her.

It was Tina's father and brother who introduced her to another oddball comedy show. She has admitted that some of her earliest memories consist of watching a strange sketch comedy titled *Monty Python's Flying Circus.* The show was produced in England. After *Monty Python* episodes ran in England, they were broadcast on the Public Broadcast System (PBS) network in the United States.

There was no character named Monty Python. Nor was there any kind of flying circus. The program consisted of six members of a comedy troupe acting in sketches. Some satirized British politics, but that did not seem to matter to American audiences. Others mixed animation with live action. Sometimes troupe members appeared in the middle of a sketch as historical figures such as Napoleon or Julius Caesar. It was surreal, or dreamlike, humor and obviously not for those who like their humor more straightforward. But it struck a chord with Tina at a very young age.

Tina also enjoyed more mainstream shows. While in elementary school, Fey liked *The Mary Tyler Moore Show* and *The Bob Newhart Show.* Mary Tyler Moore played a single woman who worked as an assistant television news producer. The comedian Bob Newhart played a married psychologist. In both shows, Moore and Newhart played the straight woman or man, or the most normal person, surrounded by eccentric and zany characters. Both Moore's and Bob Newhart's characters had distinct personalities, but the humor came from their reactions to their supporting casts. Both shows are regarded among the best sitcoms from the 1970s.

Dan Aykroyd, Jane Curtin, and Laraine Newman portray an alien family called the Coneheads in a skit on *Saturday Night Live* in the late 1970s. The groundbreaking sketch comedy show premiered in 1975, when Tina Fey was only five years old. Twenty-two years later, Fey became a writer and an actor on the show.

In the 1980s, Bob Newhart starred in a different sitcom simply called *Newhart*. In this show he was an innkeeper as well as a television host in a small Vermont town. Like his role in *The Bob Newhart Show*, Newhart's character was a straight man surrounded by colorful characters. *Newhart* is also believed by critics to be one of the 1980s' best television programs. Fey said, "The shows were so character-driven, and really, really funny."[9]

Fey admits that she caved in and watched less-regarded comedies. These included *Laverne and Shirley, Happy Days,* and *The Love Boat*. All three programs were popular with television audiences, but professional critics were not kind to them. Fey describes those shows as "sugarcoated."[10]

Fey estimated that by the time she was in fifth or seventh grade she realized she had a knack for comedy. She admitted, "The only way I could get comfortable around people was to make them laugh. I was an obedient girl, and humor was my one form of rebellion. I used comedy to deflect. Like, 'Hey, check out my zit!'—you know, making fun of yourself before someone else has a chance to."[11]

She added, "I figured out that I could ingratiate myself to people by making them laugh. Essentially, I was just trying to make them like me. But after a while it became part of my identity. I remember at the end of the year in my eighth grade algebra class, I wrote a note to my teacher that basically said, 'I know that I'm kinda a cutup and I like to crack the jokes now and again, but it's only because I struggle with math.' I was already trying to define myself as 'the jokester.'"[12]

Yet not all her fellow students saw her that way. She remembered, "There was another time when I was talking to one of my classmates and I said, 'Well, when you're a funny person like I am, it can be . . .' and he

Michael Palin in a *Monty Python's Flying Circus* sketch about Attila the Hun, a warrior from the fifth century. The odd British television program was one of the several comedies Tina Fey grew up watching.

just cut me off. 'You think you're funny? Where are you getting *that* from?'"[13]

After middle school, Fey attended Upper Darby High School. She regularly received straight As. "Fey said, "I was very studious and obedient and in a lot of activities."[14] When not in class, Fey worked on the year-book, sang with the choir, and played on the school's tennis and softball teams. She once hit a walk-off home run to win a playoff game for Upper Darby. She also took advantage of her school's drama club. When the club performed the musical *Grease*, Fey played the part of Frenchie, one of the Pink Ladies. She also acted in the school play, *Dracula*.

Fey further practiced her comedy skills by writing a regular column for her school newspaper, *The Acorn*. It was a satirical column in which she poked fun at both the faculty and her fellow students.[15] To protect her identity, Fey wrote under a pen name: "The Colonel." That is the only way she could get away with making biting comments and not get in trouble.

Fey did not have much of a social life. She did not date or go to parties. She never rebelled against her parents and was generally well-behaved in the class-room. Her former drama teacher, Harry Dietzler, said, "Tina was kind of a quiet student. Not the class clown by any means, but always giving a witty remark behind her hand. All the kids in class would laugh and wonder who it was. She'd joke around but it was always in a very background kind of way."[16]

Her newspaper column was one way she could get back at the school's most popular kids. At lunch, she sat with what she called "AP [advanced placement] brainiac nerds."[17] Together they talked behind the backs of their rival classmates. They gave them mean nicknames. Kids with long hair who were into heavy metal were called "hammers."[18] Popular, pretty girls were referred to as the "Laura Ashley Parade."[19] Laura Ashley was a Welsh clothing designer who believed women could look their best wearing traditional and conservative clothes.

Fey admits today that she was nasty in high school. She said, "Technically, I was a jealous girl. But because I was jealous, I was mean."[20] She adds, "We thought we were super cool but we were our own sad little clique."[21]

3

FIRST RATE AT SECOND CITY

Fey graduated high school in June 1988. That fall, she enrolled at the University of Virginia. Every person who enters college has to pick a major. That is the subject he or she will be taking most of their courses in. After graduation, the student usually seeks a career in his or her major subject.

Fey entered college as an English major. Many people who major in English become teachers. Some try to get jobs as writers for newspapers or Web sites. They may also try to write screenplays or books. However, the actor in Fey got the better of her. She quickly switched her major to drama.

Ideally, drama majors get jobs acting. But acting is a risky career. Very few get enough regular roles to earn a living. Many have to take second jobs, such as waiting on tables in restaurants or teaching night school. It is very common for drama majors to skip acting altogether and take jobs as high-school teachers. Of course, those lucky and talented enough to hit it big can become very wealthy and famous. But they are in the minority.

Fey wanted to both act and write. She performed in college plays, including the lead role in the famous musical *Cabaret*. She played Sally Bowles, an English singer who performs in a German night club in 1931. Since *Cabaret* is a musical, Fey had to sing a wide selection of songs. Fey downplayed her singing ability. She said she has "a birthday-party-quality voice."[1]

Fey also spent time behind the scenes in the theater department. It was not as glamorous as being onstage, but it was an important place to learn what it takes to put a play together.

Fey stated, "In college, I worked in the prop room and costume shop to learn what everyone did. If you want to be a screenwriter, take an acting class to get a sense of what you're asking actors to do. Learning other skills will help you communicate with people and respect what they do."[2]

A lot of students chose to let off steam at the many parties at the university. But Fey did not drink and skipped campus parties. To this day she is proud that she has never taken drugs.[3] Fey took her drama studies seriously. She called herself a "drama geek" and spent spare time working in the theater while fellow students were out partying.[4]

Fey used her skills and knowledge to write a short play. It was a comedy, and some of her fellow students performed in it. Fey said, "I remember . . . sitting back in the back of the theater . . . watching people laugh. I was like, 'Oh my God, this is really cool.'"[5]

During summers, she worked for a theater group back in Upper Darby for students, ages eleven through seventeen. It is called Summer Stage. She worked in the box office and wrote press releases and publicity [articles]. Her drama teacher, Harry Dietzler, said, "I assigned her to do that because I knew she liked to write."[6]

Most importantly, Fey directed plays in which the young people acted. Dietzler said, "The kids loved working for her. Once she directed *Pippi Longstocking*, and one girl, Stacy Moscotti Smith, who went on to act [professionally] still talks about Tina being her favorite director."[7]

Smith went on to act in theaters across the country. She performed in musicals such as *Cabaret*, *The Unsinkable Molly Brown*, and *Peter Pan*. Smith remembers starring in *Pippi Longstocking* under Fey's direction. Smith said, "It was my first big role aside from a play I did in fifth grade. It was the first time someone [Tina] saw more in me than I saw in myself. I remember she was a lot of fun as a director—very energetic and very relatable to us. She was very into following your instinct. She treated us not like kids."[8]

During the dress rehearsal for *Pippi Longstocking*, Stacy's braces broke and a wire became stuck on her tongue. She recalled, "I went to Tina and said I can't use my tongue. She was very calm and said let's go to the nurse and she'll take care of it. They sent me to the orthodontist and I remember walking in full costume as *Pippi Longstocking* in downtown Philadelphia. Tina probably laughed hysterically afterwards, but was very understanding about it all when it was happening."[9]

Dietzler remembered another incident he felt was typical Tina Fey. "One time she directed Hans Christian Anderson. The next play after hers was *A Disney Spectacular*. Her kids started wandering into the Disney play. They thought it was cooler. She looked [at the *A Disney Spectacular* cast] and came crying to me, saying, 'That's half my cast.' It was disappointing for her not to have the cool show. But it was in character for her, not being the blonde girl getting all the guys. I marched them back into the Hans Christian Anderson play."[10]

At the end of the season, the Summer Stage participants gave out Harry Awards, named for Harry Dietzler. The college kids did skits during the awards ceremony. Stacy Moscotti Smith said, "I remember (in a Harry Awards skit) she poked fun at the kids leaving her play. It was self-deprecating humor. I thought it was kind of cool that she could poke fun at herself."[11]

Fey was hooked on theater. She graduated from the University of Virginia in 1992. At first, she decided to continue her studies at DePaul University in Chicago. But Fey changed her mind. Instead of studying drama, she would take part in a real comedy troupe called Second City. Like DePaul University, Second City is in Chicago. Several past superstars from *Saturday Night Live* got their start at Second City. Many alumni of both Second City and *Saturday Night Live* went on to become well-respected actors in movies. These include Dan Aykroyd, Gilda Radner, Bill Murray, John Belushi, and Mike Myers.

There are also many who did not play on *Saturday Night Live* who performed at Second City and went on to great stardom, including Alan Arkin, Joan Rivers, Eugene Levy, John Candy, Steve Carell, and Stephen Colbert.

Fey had no doubts in her mind. But she did have stars in her eyes. She hoped to get on television on *Saturday Night Live* or a similar show. She was determined, saying, "I just knew I wanted to get to Chicago to study with Second City."[12]

Second City entertainers perform comedy shows on stage nightly. But more importantly for people just starting out, the staff also teaches talented people how to make the best use of their abilities. Some skills Second

City instructors teach are complex such as physical and verbal communication, and how best to come up with ideas that will work. Yet they also teach how to be a good listener and how to gain self-confidence.

In addition, the Second City staff instructs its students in the fine points of both sketch comedy and improvisational, or improv, comedy. Sketch comedy consists of routines in which a script is already written. In improvisational comedy there is no pre-written sketch. The actors are given an idea and have to make a funny routine based on nothing but that idea. The television program *Whose Line Is It Anyway?* is a prime example of improvisational comedy.

Fey rented an inexpensive apartment in a tough neighborhood. She shared her apartment with a friend from college. To support herself, she took a job at a residential YMCA. Some people came to the YMCA to exercise, while others used it as a place to stay overnight. Many residents were down on their luck and had no other place to live. The big city YMCA was an interesting place for a girl from the suburbs to work.

Her specific job was folding towels from 5:30 in the morning until 2:30 in the afternoon. After work, she would return to her apartment and often take a nap. Then at night she went to her improv classes at Second City. Fey recalled, "I made, like $7 an hour, and it was freezing in Chicago, but I was so happy. I was doing comedy with the best people in the field."[13]

Fey added, "I became immersed in the cult of improvisation. I was *very* serious about it. I was like one of those athletes trying to get into the Olympics. It was all about blind focus. I was so sure that I was doing exactly what I had been put on this earth to do, and I would have done anything to make it onto that stage. Not because of *SNL,* but because I wanted to devote my life to improv."[14]

Fey said that she preferred improv over traditional sketch comedy because in traditional comedy, she "never understood what you were supposed to be thinking when you're onstage."[15] She learned that improv is about focusing entirely on one's partner on stage. By focusing on her partner's words or actions, she felt she could create funny scenes. She believed that when doing improv, she wasn't really acting.[16] She was being herself in a make-believe situation. Fey says that doing improv also helped her polish her skills as a writer.[17] Since she was working without a script, she had to continually think of funny lines and situations.

After nine months of taking classes, one of Fey's teachers invited her to audition for Second City's more intense Second City Training Center. The Second City Training Center is one of the nation's best institutions for learning the skills of improvisation comedy, sketch comedy, and comedy writing. Only those students with the most promise are accepted. However, Tina failed the audition.

Not one to give up, Fey auditioned again about two months later. This time she was accepted. She committed herself to the year-long program, and upon completion of the training center program, she was invited to become an understudy for Second City's touring company. The actors and comedians in the touring company did not perform in Chicago on Second City's home stage. Instead, they traveled around the country, doing shows in different cities.

While on tour she could not help getting to know the other actors and staff members. Among them was Jeff Richmond, one of the directors and writers. Neither Fey nor Richmond were traditionally good-looking. Richmond is five feet and three and a half inches tall. He joked that he used to buy his suits at thrift stores because, "I realized I was the size of little old men who were dying."[18] Fey stands five feet and four and a half inches tall and at the time weighed about one hundred fifty pounds.[19] She had a short, boyish haircut, far from the shoulder-length cut she has become famous for.

Richmond did not mind that Fey was a little on the pudgy side. He found her very attractive. He described her as "a lovely turn-of-the-century kind of round—that beautiful, Rubenesque kind of beauty."[20] (Peter Paul Rubens was a seventeenth-century Flemmish painter known for depicting full-figured women.)

Fey and her husband, Jeff Richmond, in 2004.

In addition, Richmond recalled that Fey wore comfortable clothes that did not always match. She was often seen around the theater wearing boots, knee-length matronly dresses, and sweaters one would buy at thrift stores. Yet Richmond found even her unusual wardrobe attractive in its own way. He said, "It still looked kind of cool on her."[21]

Fey and Richmond had much more in common than funky dressing. They liked the same kind of offbeat humor. They often had lunch together and seemed to live on a diet of hot dogs and hamburgers. On one date, they went to the Museum of Science and Industry in Chicago and walked through a huge model of a human heart. Before long, the two were a couple.

Richmond remembered, "I fell in love with her very quickly."[22]

After traveling with the road company for about eight months, Fey was given the opportunity to perform on Second City's main stage in Chicago. At her peak she was doing eight shows a week. She became good friends with several of her fellow performers such as Amy Poehler, Rachel Dratch, and Horatio Sanz.

In one sketch Fey played a mother to a teenage daughter played by Dratch. The two are having an argument. Fey as the mother yells at Dratch as the teenage daughter, "You're just like your father. . . . You smell like your father." The audience laughed. Then Dratch's character replied, "The only reason I smell like my father is because you won't let me wear perfume and I have to wear Old Spice."[23] (Old Spice is an aftershave made for men.) The audience roared in laughter.

Dratch laughed when she discussed the art of improv comedy: "You don't know what's going to come out of your mouth. You don't know what's going to come out of your partner's mouth. It's just like an amusement park ride or something." She then quickly added, "When it goes well."[24]

Not everything worked for Fey. She experimented with standup comedy. In standup, the comedian stands by him or herself on stage in front of a live audience and tells pre-written jokes. There are different types of standup. Superstars such as Bill Cosby to Chris Rock began doing standup. Comedians like Cosby specialized in long, funny stories. Those like Rock did their best with one-liners, or jokes that consist of one humorous line.

Fey said she tried performing standup during open-mic [microphone] nights. On open-mic nights, amateurs are allowed to tell their jokes or humorous stories on stage. Fey felt she was not very good at it, but she added that perhaps she did not give it a real chance. She admitted, "But I really admire standup, and I think I would have loved to learn how to do it. I think it's terrifying and thrilling. A really cool thing to do."[25]

Fey summed up her time with Second City by joking about improvisation. She smiled, "Well, I think it's really good for people who are lazy. You can't prepare. You'd be cheating if you prepared."[26]

She then became serious and added, "For me, improvisation was a nice mix of the actor's brain and the writer's brain working together. For me, Second City and improvisation in general completely changed my life. It defined for me the kind of work I wanted to do, the way in which I could still be a performer."[27]

She noted that learning how to perform for an audience in a more traditional method would have never worked for her. "I would not have made it and I'd be teaching English in high school somewhere (right now)."[28]

By 1997, Fey had spent several years with Second City. She thought it was time to put all those lessons she had learned to good use.

4

LONG DAYS AT
SATURDAY NIGHT LIVE

In 1997, staff members from *Saturday Night Live* approached members of Second City's cast looking for fresh talent. *SNL* has had much luck with former members of Second City. In a way, Second City became like a minor-league team for a major-league baseball team. *SNL* was the major leagues.

One of the *SNL* staff members then was former Second City member Adam McKay. In 1997, he was *Saturday Night Live*'s head writer, or the supervisor of the writing staff. McKay remembered Fey from his stint with Second City. He thought she might be a good addition to *SNL*'s writing staff. Even though McKay and Fey were friends, Tina had to apply for the job.

McKay told her to take time in the summer of 1997 to work on some comedy sketches. He told her to send him six of them. Each was to be ten pages long. Fey spent the summer working on the sketches. Long-time *Saturday Night Live* producer Lorne Michaels looked them over. He had to make a decision: were they good enough for Fey to work on a famous television program?

Michaels liked what he read. He and Fey arranged to meet each other. Just a week later, Fey was offered a job as a staff writer on *SNL*. She would be one of the few female writers on the staff.

On one hand, Fey was offered to do what she always dreamed of. On the other hand, it was terrifying because there would be a lot of pressure to live up to *SNL*'s high standards. She called fellow Second City member Amy Poehler and started crying on the phone. Poehler convinced Fey not to throw away the opportunity to work with the best at *Saturday Night Live*.

Fey said, "Then the ladies from Second City took me out to dinner at this awesome restaurant in Chicago called Wishbone. I got up from the table because I had to vomit from pure nerves. I've never had that before in my life."[1]

She took Poehler's advice and accepted the job. Despite her nervousness, in one way it was relaxing. Fey admitted, "When I got there (*Saturday Night Live*) after doing eight shows a week at Second City it was like a nice vacation."[2]

Jimmy Fallon, Rachel Dratch, and actor Ray Liotta perform
a Fun Friends Club sketch on *Saturday Night Live* in 2003.

Soon she realized there is a huge difference between doing improv at Second City and writing for a television show that does sketch comedy. She said, "When I was told to sit down at your computer and write something and turn it in, I kind of froze up because I wasn't used to sitting down and writing things. I was used to improvising and re-improvising. So that took a couple of weeks getting used to writing things by myself."[3]

She also had to get used to *SNL*'s weekly schedule. Monday is usually the day to meet the guest host. Also, on Monday, the staff discusses the news events of the week and thinks about which would be the basis for funny sketches. Tuesday is the busiest day for the writers. They spend Tuesday writing the entire show. The scripts are due on Wednesday.

Fey said that the toughest day for a beginning writer is Wednesday. On Wednesday, the whole staff meets in one room. They then have a read-through, in which the writers read aloud sketches they wrote. It is a test to discover which sketches work and which ones do not.

Fey remarked, "When you first come to *Saturday Night Live* as a writer, it is a very stressful, nerve-wracking experience . . . because your first sketch is never going to go that well because you don't know the lay of the land yet and people don't know you yet. And it's a red hot kind of embarrassment that starts in your stomach and just flushes through your body in waves.

But between Second City and here (*SNL*) you build a good tolerance to embarrassment."[4]

She added, "It's a tough room and they've heard a *lot* of comedy over the years. The first time you get a laugh in that room is really exciting."[5]

First scripts are never perfect. The staff spends Thursday rewriting and perfecting sketches. That can take up to twelve hours. Fridays are devoted to what is called blocking. In blocking, the director and actors decide where the actors will stand and move on stage. That is necessary so the camera persons and lighting technicians will know how to adjust their equipment.

Saturday is the day for rehearsals. When a sketch is being rehearsed, the writer who created it sits next to *SNL* executive producer Lorne Michaels. Michaels takes notes as each sketch is rehearsed. He may suggest or demand last minute changes.

There are commonly more men than women writers for *Saturday Night Live*. However, Fey said she felt no discrimination. According to Fey, it is all about talent. She compared sketch comedy writing to playing basketball. If someone passes the ball to you and you make the basket, your teammates will pass the ball to you again. If you write good comedy material, then your fellow staff members will go back to you when they need more ideas.

It took a few weeks for Fey's first sketch to make it on the air. It featured overweight cast member Chris

Dratch and Fallon play Denise and Sully in a 2000 episode of *SNL*.

Farley as an overgrown baby on a serious television talk show. Within a few more weeks she came up with sketch ideas that worked very well. Several became the basis for recurring sketches, those that feature the same characters in different situations.

She often wrote parodies, or comic versions, of the daily all-female talk show, *The View.* She once developed a sketch about the Fun Friends Club, a kids' show similar to *Barney and Friends.* All the "actors" on the Fun Friends Club are small children except Rachel Dratch. Dratch plays a woman who long ago was a kid actor on the Fun Friends Club. Because the show is so much fun, she has refused to leave. Because of her age, she sticks out like a wart.

Another favorite recurring sketch Fey wrote with Dratch featured two fictional teenagers from suburban Boston named Sully and Denise. Though Fey was from the Philadelphia area, the sketch seemed perfect for Dratch, who grew up outside of Boston. Dratch played Denise and cast member Jimmy Fallon played Sully.

As an exaggeration of teenage romances, Sully and Denise would insult each other, then make up within seconds. Both characters were diehard fans of the Boston Red Sox, and Sully's favorite player was Nomar Garciaparra. In the late 1990s, Garciaparra was the all-star shortstop for the Red Sox. Sully paid tribute to Garciaparra in so many sketches that one time, the real Nomar Garciaparra played himself on the show.

great reviews. Even the conservative *Wall Street Journal* raved, "Indeed, the fun part of watching these two perform together is seeing how comfortable they are with each other, as if they are in somebody's basement putting on a show for a bunch of friends. It's also interesting to see two very funny women working as a team. Interesting because there have been so few two-woman comedy teams."[8]

Rachel Dratch impersonates Harry Potter on "Weekend Update" with Tina Fey and Jimmy Fallon, November 17, 2001.

The review concluded, "But 'Dratch & Fey' isn't about two women being funny. Any more than Abbott and Costello got laughs because they were a couple of guys. Dratch and Fey are just funny. Period."[9]

When fall closed in, it was time to return to New York City and *Saturday Night Live*. The 2000–2001 season of *SNL* was going to be different. Fey planned to continue only as a writer.[10] However, Lorne Michaels thought Fey had a very good acting chemistry with cast member Jimmy Fallon. He wanted Fey and Fallon to replace Colin Quinn as news anchors in the show's "Weekend Update" portion. That is the segment that takes place midway through each *Saturday Night Live* episode. The anchor, or anchors, satirize the weekly news.

Fey never auditioned for the part on "Weekend Update." She said that Michaels was impressed with Dratch and Fey's live show the previous summer. Fey noted, "It was Lorne's idea for me and Jimmy to test together to do 'Update.'"[11]

Fallon remembered that Michaels went up to him and said, "'Tina's going to be the smart, brainy girl, and you're going to be the kind of goofy guy that doesn't do his homework and asks her for answers and stuff.' You know, Lorne is brilliant with that stuff. So it was like, 'Okay, I like it.'

"We did a test with just me, Tina, the cameramen, a director, and Lorne. And after one take, he would come out with, 'Okay, relax a little bit more.' And, 'I like Tina on this side and Jim on this side.' Lorne said, 'What we'll do is, we'll do it until Christmas, because it takes a long time to get into it, and if you hate it or it's not working, we can find something else.'"[12]

Even though Fey did not come up with the idea of playing anchorwoman, she took the chance. The pairing of Fallon and Fey worked beautifully. Comedian and political analyst Dennis Miller, who years before had played a "Weekend Update" anchor, said, "Tina Fey might be the best 'Weekend Update' who ever did it. She writes the funniest jokes."[13] And Tina Fey had a new job she had not expected—television actor and comedian.

5

"DREAM JOBS TO PEOPLE—BUT THEY ARE ALSO VERY HARD"

Soon Fey was known to television viewers as the smart, funny, and pretty girl with the dark-rimmed glasses who did the fake news on *Saturday Night Live*. Some thought her glasses made her look smart. They soon became her trademark.

It would have surprised her many fans to learn that the glasses were not hers. Fey wore contact lenses. She needs to wear them to read cue cards—big cards on which the actors' dialogue and jokes are written. The actors read their lines off cue cards while the show is on the air. Fey's glasses were merely a stage prop.

Fey recounted that during one episode of *Saturday Night Live* she did not wear her glasses for "Weekend Update" because right afterward, she had to appear in a sketch that did not call for them. Fey did the "Weekend Update" segment while wearing her contact lenses. Her followers did not like that change. Posters on fan sites wanted her to put the glasses back on. She did.

Jimmy Fallon had his followers, too. But Fey was the star of the duo. Journalist Heidi Mitchell wrote: "That Fey wrote her own material only added to her appeal: men wanted to date this cute hilarious nerd; women wanted to be her."[1] Fey had accidentally stumbled onto a secret. One did not have to be drop-dead gorgeous to be attractive. Taking care of herself and being intelligent made Fey attractive.

Because she does not wear glasses in public, Fey rarely is recognized by her fans. Writer Jason Gay cleverly called it, "a reverse Clark Kent effect."[2] Clark Kent was the real name of comic-book character Superman. He wore glasses in public so he would not be recognized as the caped superhero.

The new "Weekend Update" was a huge success. At the same time, the entire show, *Saturday Night Live*, was getting wows from the critics once again. During the early and mid-1990s, television reviewers had said that *SNL* was no longer funny. However, Fey is an extremely modest person. To that end, she has continually refused to take the credit for the show's rebound. Instead, she said the show's critical raves or pans have more to do with the fickleness of the fans and television reporters.

Fey explained, "Reaction to the show seems to go through cycles, and it's entirely random. A few years go by and some hack [unskilled] journalist gets the idea to write another article with the title 'Saturday Night Dead.' Then five lazy writers follow his lead, and it becomes a foregone conclusion that the show's doomed. I don't think I'm more deserving of praise than anybody else who ever had this job. I just got lucky."[3]

In spite of her success in front of the camera, Fey maintained that performers are nowhere without good writers. She stressed to young people that the television industry needs people to compose the words actors say. When asked what advice she has for young talented women, she resplied, "At *SNL*, when you come downstairs to leave after the show, there are people waiting for autographs. A lot of the young women I talked to there told me they wanted to be writers. I always tried to encourage them. I think the world has too many actresses."[4]

Fey often worked on sketches and "Weekend Update" material every morning through the night until the early hours of the next morning. Sometimes she would stay up until 5 A.M. writing and rewriting material. During her time as a "Weekend Update" anchor, she once sighed, "Even now, I wish I had a little craft shop somewhere in Florida,'"[5] Her boyfriend, Jeff Richmond, noted, "Every job she has had has been a great job—they are dream jobs to people—but they are also very hard."[6]

On one occasion, Fey took a vacation with Richmond on the shores of Lake Michigan. They had been dating for seven years. One day, Richmond went in front of Fey, dropped down to one knee, and asked her to marry him. It was a very traditional way of proposing. Of course, Fey said yes. It was a happy occasion, but Richmond jokes about one regret. Since Fey became famous, people have asked him many times how he proposed to her. Fey stated, "My husband always said, 'If I'd known so many people would ask me how I proposed, I would have done it in a more theatrical way.'"[7]

Their wedding took place on June 3, 2001, in Philadelphia. Following a ceremony in the Greek Orthodox tradition, the couple went all out with a big, splashy party. The couple and their guests danced to the music of a twelve-piece dance band.

After the wedding, Fey and Richmond settled in a New York City apartment. It would be convenient for her to get to work at NBC's office building at 30 Rockefeller Center.

In the fall, the annual Emmy Awards were held. Fey and the *Saturday Night Live* staff were nominated for outstanding writing for a variety, music, or comedy program. They did not win, however, losing to *The Daily Show With John Stewart.*

However, Fey and her crew did win an award given by the Writers Guild of America (WGA). The WGA is a labor union, or organization that supports the rights of radio, television, and movie writers. Fey's award was for her work on the *Saturday Night Live 25th Anniversary Special.*

Lorne Michaels said, "There's a group of people who feel Tina can do no wrong in my eyes. But that's because she's just wrong less often than other people."[8]

After the 2001–2002 of *SNL,* Fey was ready to try something new to test her writing skills: a full movie screenplay. But what would she write about?

She remembered reading an article in the *New York Times* that caught her eye. It was about a then new book titled *Queen Bees and Wannabes: Helping Your Daughter Survive Cliques, Gossip, Boyfriends, and Other Realities of Adolescence.* The book's author is educator Rosalind Wiseman. Fey brought the article to the attention of Lorne Michaels. It reminded Fey of her years in high school. She thought it might be a good basis for a movie. She said, "The stuff Rosalind talks about rang true to me."[9]

Queen Bees and Wannabes was hardly the type of book that can easily be made into a screenplay. Most books adapted into screenplays are novels with basic story lines. *Queen Bees and Wannabes* is a nonfiction self-help book. It does not tell a story. Its purpose is to give parents advice on raising daughters through what can be troublesome teenage years. How would Fey convert such a book into a screenplay?

Fey admitted, "If it had been a novel, it would have been easier—to just adapt the book straight. But I sort of had to take the ideas, take the character types that Rosalind lays out in the book. And I did talk to a few girls here and there on my own and just figure out a way to use those in the story."[10]

Fey and Michaels discussed the idea fully. If they did make a movie, they would be working together. After several years of doing so, they had become a good team. Fey would write the screenplay and Michaels would produce the movie, which meant he would be in charge of supervising the entire project. That would include finding a studio to spend millions of dollars to make the movie.

Both Fey and Michaels read Wiseman's book. They believed that even though it is nonfiction, it has elements of comedy. Fey also thought back to her high-school days, recalling how mean she and her friends in her clique were. Fey admitted, "High school girls are ingenious in how they sabotage one another in these invisible, unseen, hurtful ways. The way they mess with each other is so clever and intricate."[11]

Fey also did some research on her own. To learn what was on teenage girls' minds, she read magazines written for them. She studied numerous Web sites devoted to teenage girls. Fey also took time to go to local shopping malls and watch how teenagers inter-acted. She compared some of their behavior to that of animals in the wild. She laughed. "It's like animals grooming themselves at the watering hole."[12]

Fey also worked with Wiseman. She promised Wiseman that she would not turn her book into a "stupid, cheesy teen comedy."[13] Wiseman wanted any movie based on her book to have intelligence as well as humor.

Fey then got busy writing. She was in for a tough lesson. Creating a full-length movie screenplay is much different than writing short sketches. Fey conceded, "It was hard. It was so much longer than a sketch. No one told me it would have to be so much longer." She laughed. "And you have to tell a story for ninety minutes."[14] Fey finished her first draft of the movie script in the summer of 2002. By this time, her script had a title: *Mean Girls.*

At that fall's Emmy Awards, she was again nomi-nated for outstanding writing for a variety, music, or comedy program for her work on *Saturday Night Live.* Unlike the 2001 Emmys, this time she and her staff won. It was the first award *SNL* had won in that category in more than ten years.[15]

Fey continued to write sketches for *SNL* and serve as coanchor for "Weekend Update" during the 2002–2003 season. The regular *Saturday Night Live* schedule kept her so busy that she could not give her screenplay much attention. Every first draft needs work. Plotlines must be altered. Dialogue needs to be sharpened. Characters have to be better defined.

While Fey did not have a lot of time to work on rewriting the script during the *SNL* season, she and Michaels were able to proceed with certain decisions. They were able to get a major movie industry studio, Paramount Pictures, to purchase the rights to Wiseman's book. That means the studio paid Wiseman money to use her book as the basis for the movie.

Because Wiseman is the author of *Queen Bees and Wannabes,* it is only fair that she received a payment for allowing others to use her book to make money. Paramount Pictures then made a commitment to make the movie. That is a major achievement. Many screenplays are purchased by studios but they do not get made into movies.

Word then got out among people in the motion-picture business about this teenage movie that was not going to be just another teenage movie. Michaels hired Mark Waters to direct *Mean Girls.* The director supervises the actors and crew during the filming. He or she may tell an actor to put more emotion into a scene. Or he or she might let a camera operator know that a close-up rather than a long shot is needed in a certain scene. Waters had just completed the movie *Freaky Friday* starring Lindsay Lohan and Jamie Lee Curtis. It had not yet been released to the public, but Michaels

Tina Fey in her trademark glasses, *SNL* creator Lorne Michaels, and writer Dennis McNicholas hold their Emmys for outstanding writing for a variety, music, or comedy program, in 2002.

and Fey had seen an early version of it. They liked the way Waters directed it.[16]

In the spring of 2003, Lohan attended a broadcast of *Saturday Night Live*. She had seen a draft of the script and expressed interest in acting in it. Based on her acting in *Freaky Friday*, Michaels and Fey thought she was the right actor to play the main character, Cady Herron.

Fey was given permission to rewrite the script by herself. That is unusual for a first-time screenwriter. Much of the time, professional and experienced screen-writers are hired to put final touches on a beginner's screenplay. It was a tribute to Fey that she was allowed to complete the rewrite on her own. "Lorne was very protective of me," Fey said.[17] She spent the summer in a beach community called Fire Island in New York City. There she had the peace and quiet to polish her screenplay.

6

THE MAKING OF A LANDMARK MOVIE

In the fall of 2003, Fey was once again writing for a new season of *Saturday Night Live*. And as before, she was performing as coanchor on the "Weekend Update" segment.

About this time, Fey returned to Upper Darby High School to speak to students. News anchor Katie Couric interviewed her. While the students wanted to know about her work at *Saturday Night Live*, Harry Dietzler and some other teachers had another question in mind. "We told Katie to ask Tina if she was The Colonel, who wrote for the school newspaper, *The Acorn,* years ago. It was the best kept secret in the school for twenty years. She admitted she was. The secret was finally out."[1]

Meanwhile, the filming of *Mean Girls* had begun in Toronto, Ontario, Canada. Fey found time to break from her busy *Saturday Night Live* schedule to fly to Toronto often to work with the actors and other staff.

Michaels praised Fey's dedication to the movie, despite the fact that she was exhausted from her *SNL* work. Michaels said, "Making a movie with somebody is like driving cross-country. You have to have a lot of respect for them because there's going to be times when you want to not be in the car. Tina, she's brilliant. She has a standard and she's not going to compromise it."[2]

The plotline of *Mean Girls* went like this. Cady Heron, played by Lindsay Lohan, is sixteen years old. She has just moved to a suburb of Chicago. Cady's parents are research scientists. For all of Cady's childhood, she lived with her parents in a remote part of Africa where her parents worked with animals. Because there were no schools nearby, Cady was homeschooled by her parents.

Now that she is living in the United States, she will be attending a public high school for the first time. The experience is alien to her. She has always been allowed to act independently. Suddenly she has teachers telling her when she can and cannot be out of her seat. In the beginning of the movie, she has trouble finding a place to sit in her homeroom. While looking for a seat, she walks in the front of her classroom and accidentally bumps into her homeroom teacher, Ms. Norbury, played by Fey. Ms. Norbury ends up spilling

Lindsay Lohan as Cady Heron and Tina Fey as Ms. Norbury in 2004's *Mean Girls*.

coffee all over herself. As Ms. Norbury, Fey wore her trademark dark-rimmed glasses.

In time, Cady becomes friends with a troubled girl named Janis and a gay boy named Damian. Janis and Damian are friends and are part of a clique called the art freaks.

Shortly afterward, Cady is invited to sit at lunch with Regina, Gretchen, and Karen. They are the three most popular girls in school. Regina is the leader, or "queen bee." Gretchen and Karen are her "worker bees." They also happen to be the meanest girls in school. Janis and Damian refer to Regina, Gretchen, and Karen as the plastics. *Plastic* is a slang term for fake.

At first, Regina, Gretchen, and Karen are nice to Cady. Regina knows that Cady is naïve and unused to a real school. So she becomes friends with Cady and tries to make Cady into a popular girl like herself. Soon there are complications in their new friendship. Regina finds out that Cady likes her old boyfriend, Aaron Samuels. Cady also learns that Janis and Regina—as opposite as they are in high school—had been friends in middle school. When Regina started to outgrow Janis and hang around with her first boyfriend, Janis felt left out. Janis continued to call Regina to get together. Regina mistook her interest as a romantic attraction. Regina began spreading rumors that Janis is a lesbian.

Left to right, Lacey Chabert, Rachel McAdams, Lindsay Lohan, and Amanda Seyfried in the "Jingle Bell Rock" dance scene from *Mean Girls*.

Janis continues to tell Cady how mean Regina is. But naïve Cady finds Regina to be nice. Then at a Halloween party, Regina decides she wants Aaron to be her boyfriend again. She kisses Aaron in front of Cady. Cady now understands Regina's true nature. She goes to Janis's house where Janis and Damian are watching television. Cady tells Janis what happened at the party. Janis decides it is time to bring Regina down a peg. Janis, Damian, and Cady plot revenge against Regina.

The movie delves into the insecurities of girls in high school. Late in the movie, Gretchen admits to Cady that Regina is mean to her, too. Regina snubs Gretchen at times, and she dictates to Gretchen what she can wear. But Gretchen feels it is better to be part of the popular group than to be left out, even if she is abused.

Fey took a lot of care in writing the screenplay. The name Regina is Latin for "queen." Although Fey used Wiseman's book as a basis for the screenplay, she also dug into her own past when she came up with unflattering names for different cliques.

Fey said Regina is not based on any one person. Regina is a composite character, or a character based on different parts of several girls' personalities—all girls who threatened her in high school. Fey even admitted that Regina's character also included a bit of her own personality. "I was a real snarky girl," Fey conceded.[3] She recalled that she had a crush on a boy who had a crush on another girl. Fey said she spent "a lot of wasted hours just badmouthing another girl that had never really done anything to me, except be better-looking than me. That was her only crime."[4]

It turns out there was some real-life drama going on behind the scenes of *Mean Girls*. Star Lindsay Lohan, who was seventeen, was involved in a feud with teen star Hillary Duff over a teenaged-boy celebrity. It made news in gossip magazines. Fey used the occasion to blast those magazines for publishing stories about teen actors' private lives. Fey said, "Sometimes I think Us Weekly should leave them alone. They're just kids. If notes I wrote about some girl in ninth grade were in Us Weekly, I'd really be bummed."[5]

When the movie was made, Lindsay Lohan was the only big name actor in it. The parts of Gretchen, Karen, Janis, Damian, and Aaron were played by then little-known actors. Since then, many have gone on to big careers. After *Mean Girls*, Rachel McAdams, who plays Regina, acted in *Wedding Crashers*, *The Notebook*, and *The Time Traveler's Wife*. Lacey Chabert, who plays Gretchen, costarred in *Ghosts of Girlfriends Past*. Amanda Seyfried, who plays Karen, had a recurring role in the hit cable series *Big Love* and starred in the movie version of *Mamma Mia*.

Three other actors were Fey's current or former costars on *Saturday Night Live*. Amy Poehler plays Regina's mother, who is just like a grown-up version of Regina. Former *SNL* actor Tim Meadows plays the school principal, and Ana Gasteyer plays Cady's mother. Although Rachel McAdams and Amy Poehler play daughter and mother, in real life they are just seven years apart. McAdams was born in 1978 and Poehler was born in 1971.[6] Yet through makeup, a sharp casting decision, and fine acting, they seem perfect as daughter and mother.

Although both Fey and Michaels had high hopes for the movie, they had no idea what audiences would think. It is common for new movies and television programs to be played in front of specially selected audiences, called focus groups, before being released to the public. The focus groups are then asked what they liked or did not like about the movie. *Mean Girls* producer Lorne Michaels said, "There were focus groups of people who were high school age and they kept saying that this is like my high school. And that's when I think I began to realize we were close [to what we were trying to achieve]."[7]

Fey was concerned that the movie would appeal just to girls. She wondered if boys would want to see it.[8]

There was nothing to be concerned about. *Mean Girls* was a smash. It was released into theaters on April 30, 2004. The movie had cost $17 million to make.[9] In the first weekend alone it had earned over $24 million, a clear profit.[10] About 75 percent of the people who watched it that weekend were female, while 50 percent of the audiences were under age eighteen.[11] More than 90 percent of the audience rated the movie either "excellent" or "very good."[12] Yet even those outside the target audience, like men in their thirties, loved it. A total of 80 percent of those men described the movie as "excellent" or "very good."[13]

Professional critics raved. Ann Hornaday of the *Washington Post* wrote, "'*Mean Girls*' boasts a one-two-three punch in star Lindsay Lohan, screenwriter Tina Fey and director Mark Waters, and, indeed, it delivers a knockout."[14] The *Seattle Times* critic Moira McDonald beamed, "It's really the dialogue, sharp as a perfectly manicured fingernail, that deserves top billing here. And within those funny lines are a few nonpreachy thoughts about self-acceptance that teenage girls would do well to heed. Tart and refreshing, '*Mean Girls*' is the kind of high-school movie that really feels as if it's for grown-ups—but hey, the teens can come, too."[15] Movie reviewer Nev Pierce of the highly respected British Broadcasting Company wrote: "And while the story may be fictional, the setting feels authentic. Fey clearly remembers how cruel kids can be, and the crippling desire to be cool at school—whether through jargon, dress-sense, or doing someone else down. The script is witty, barbed, and, crucially, true."[16]

Rosalind Wiseman, author of the book on which the movie was based, had a milder reaction. She said, "I've had many kids around the country say to me that

that was their high school, but certainly that is not all kids. Some kids would say that in no way that was like their experience. And both are equally valid. Both are equally true."[17]

The movie played throughout the summer, into September. Fans went to see it two, three, or four times. One scene, with Cady and the plastics dancing to "Jingle Bell Rock" at the school's Winter Talent Show, became an instant classic. Girls, and even female teachers, at real high schools still perform it at their school talent shows.

Mean Girls earned more than $86 million in the United States and more than $42 million more in foreign theaters.[18] Few movies are both praised by the majority of critics and financial successes. *Mean Girls* accomplished both. The movie has gone on to become a mini-classic and made Tina Fey a household name—even for those who do not watch *Saturday Night Live*.

7

LIZ AND JACK IN THE TELEVISION WORLD

ean Girls cemented Fey's reputation as more than the woman who does the fake news on *Saturday Night Live*. Meanwhile, Fey was working with NBC on another idea. While actor Alec Baldwin was not a regular on *Saturday Night Live*, he was the closest thing to one. He was guest host twelve times.[1] Baldwin and Fey were close friends.

In 2004, Baldwin did an interview with Fey for a magazine appropriately called *Interview*. Baldwin asked Fey what she was working on next. Fey answered, "I don't know. I'm supposed to be developing something for NBC, but I don't know what it's going to be yet. I was going to call you about my first idea, but then I changed ideas. I was working on a sitcom, and I was going to call and ask if you wanted to play a Bill O'Reilly type, but

I changed the whole thing."[2] Bill O'Reilly is a very conservative talk-show host for the Fox News television network. Unlike O'Reilly, Baldwin is known for having very liberal political views. It would have been an interesting role for Baldwin to play.

As Fey continued to think of ideas for a future NBC project, she went back to her old job at *SNL* in the fall of 2004. However, there was one major change. Her coanchor of four years, Jimmy Fallon, left the show in May. Fey did not find out who her new "Weekend Update" coanchor would be until one week before the new season started on October 2, 2004.[3] It turned out to be her old friend Amy Poehler. This marked the first time in the history of *Saturday Night Live* that two women anchored "Weekend Update."[4]

Producer Lorne Michaels confessed that it was a gamble to pair Fey and Poehler, but not because they are women. He said it was because Fallon and Fey were so popular and worked so well together that "anyone following Jimmy and Tina was a risk."[5]

Fey said that she and Poehler acted naturally as coanchors. They were sarcastic but also easygoing. Fey admitted that attitude "is our real dynamic. We are real friends and really like each other. And Amy is genuinely a cool girl."[6] Both fans and critics accepted the new duo and generally gave them thumbs up.

In the past, young stars of *Saturday Night Live* had gotten well-deserved reputations as big partiers.

Fey and Poehler in a 2005 "Weekend Update" sketch.

But success did not change Tina Fey. She was the same person she was in college. When not at work, she spent most of her time with her husband. During downtime at work, she and Poehler hung around together like the two longtime friends they are. Poehler said, "Tina and I play board games. We're so boring. I love reading decorating magazines and watching decorating shows."[7]

In the meantime, Fey was still thinking about ideas for her future television project. One idea hit her—what about a fictional television show about a television show? It had been done before. *The Mary Tyler Moore Show* was one. *Murphy Brown,* which ran from 1988 to 1998, was about life at a nationally broadcast television news magazine program similar to *60 Minutes.*

Fey had her own specific idea, *30 Rock.* The managers at NBC liked the idea and gave her a go-ahead in the spring of 2005.

Fey plays Liz Lemon, the head writer of a program titled *The Girlie Show,* or *TGS* for short. The star of *TGS* is Jenna Maroney, a stuck-up but insecure actress. *TGS* is a success, but then a new executive director named Jack Donaghy, played by Alec Baldwin, is transferred to work on it. Jack's previous job had nothing to do with the creative side of television. The fact that he is clueless regarding the workings of television causes him to make unwise changes to *TGS.* Jack's first step is to hire eccentric movie star Tracy Jordan to costar with Jenna on *TGS*. Jack's reason is that he wants to get more men to watch the show. Jack then changes the show's name to *The Girlie Show With Tracy Jordan*. That is despite the fact that the character, Tracy Jordan, is a man.

There are several other characters, including writers, actors, and Kenneth, the naïve page who moved from a small town to New York. But Liz, Jack, Jenna, and Tracy are the main characters.

Even though Baldwin does not play a Bill O'Reilly type of talk-show host, Jack Donaghy is similar to the real Bill O'Reilly. Both are very conservative politically. Some observers feel that Donaghy's attitude and mannerisms are similar to O'Reilly's. Fey asked her *SNL* costar of several years, Tracy Morgan, to play Tracy Jordan. Morgan accepted. Lorne Michaels and *Saturday Night Live*'s coproducer Marci Klein agreed to take over the controls as executive producers.

Fey's first choice to play Jenna Maroney was her friend Rachel Dratch. Dratch played Jenna in the pilot episode of *30 Rock*. The pilot is the first episode of a television show. It is a sort of test episode. In this case, it was decided that Dratch was not the right person to play Jenna. Fey said the original decision to replace Dratch was not hers, but it was her responsibility to defend it.[8]

Fey made a personal phone call to Dratch to tell her she was being replaced. Fey said that Dratch "was very cool about it. Dratch said, 'Believe me, if this was anybody else's show, I would have just been fired.' It ended up being a good decision in the long run."[9] Dratch has since been cast on the show to play different, quirky characters. Some writers in the entertainment media reported that Dratch had been demoted. Dratch responded, "Well, when Tina told me I was going to play different characters each show, I was actually psyched about it, because it sounded really unique. But then the media kind of ran with this 'demotion' thing, so that was kind of a bummer. But whatever, I'm over it."[10]

In addition to her new program, Fey had one more addition to her busy life. She gave birth to a baby daughter on September 10, 2005. The little girl's name is Alice Zenobia Richmond. Alice's middle name is in honor of Fey's mother. Fey took a maternity leave, or a break from working, from *SNL* right after Alice was born. *SNL* cast member Horatio Sanz replaced her on "Weekend Update" until Fey returned on October 22.

With a new member of her family and a television show in the works, Fey could not continue her schedule. The 2005-2006 season was her last as a regular *Saturday Night Live* cast member. She said, "You can't stay at *Saturday Night Live* forever. It's a little like trying to stay in high school forever. You need to move on, and you need to let somebody else

30 Rock premiered Wednesday, October 11, 2006, at 8:00 P.M. Plotlines that season had to do with a wide range of subjects. In an early episode, Liz tries but fails to keep *The Girlie Show* staff happy; crazy Tracy comes to the rescue when he holds a party for the *TGS* cast and crew on a big yacht. In another episode, Jenna is scheduled to appear on the television show, *Late Night With Conan O'Brien.* But Jack decides to put Tracy on instead of Jenna. To make things worse, Tracy has gone off medication that controls his mood swings. That makes him even more unpredictable when he appears on O'Brien's show. Another episode poked fun at the idea of product placement. Product placement is a technique advertisers use to get free publicity. They arrange to have their products placed on the sets of actual television programs.

Not all the plots had to do with business. Many focused on personal relationships. Some had to do with Liz's dating life. Others focused on problems Jack has with his mother, a very controlling woman. Midway through the first season, Jack divorces his wife in what had been a strained marriage. That opened up a whole world of possibilities with Jack dating different women.

The first four episodes of *30 Rock* had few viewers. So the fifth episode was moved from Wednesday at 8 P.M. to Thursday, November 16, at 9:30 P.M. For more than twenty years NBC had had good luck with hit situation comedies on Thursday. These included *The*

Cosby Show, Family Ties, Cheers, Seinfeld, and *Friends.* With the move to Thursday, *30 Rock*'s ratings were a bit higher than on Wednesday. Ultimately, *30 Rock* was moved a half hour earlier, and in early January it began airing at 9 P.M. The number of viewers was adequate but not great.

The ratings for *Studio 60 on the Sunset Strip,* the other fictional show about *Saturday Night Live,* were better than those of *30 Rock.* But critics had mixed reviews of *Studio 60.* Some said it tried to be both a comedy and drama. While some television programs succeed with that mix, *Studio 60* was not successful. Other critics said *Studio 60* took its characters too seriously. After all, it was supposed to be about a comedy show. Critic James Poniewozik compared *30 Rock* and *Studio 60* this way: "*30 Rock* is willing to let each of its characters be right and wrong; it's confident we don't need to worship them to like them."[14]

As early as the month of November, television reporter Roger Friedman commented that *Studio 60* was not going to last.[15] Even though *Studio 60* had more viewers than *30 Rock,* its total numbers had been disappointing. The program broadcast that was on before *Studio 60* was a new science-fiction drama called *Heroes.* About half of the viewers of *Heroes* did not stick around to watch *Studio 60.*[16] Friedman said that *Studio 60* failed because television audiences did not find the characters interesting.[17]

A scene from the 2008 film *Baby Mama* starring Tina Fey and Amy Poehler.

In the summer of 2007, Fey told a press conference, or a gathering of reporters, that she was "100 percent" certain that *30 Rock* would outlast *Studio 60*.[18] Then an hour later, she told a reporter what she should have said was "100 percent—and there's a 50 percent chance I could have been wrong."[19]

But Fey was right. *30 Rock* was renewed for another season. That was despite the fact that out of 142 prime-time network shows, *30 Rock* finished in 102nd place.[20] However, the show received ten nominations for Emmy awards, a sure sign of excellence.[21] NBC Entertainment President Kevin Reilly said the network expects the show to "continue to build its increasingly loyal audience and become another of NBC's classic comedy series."[22]

Meanwhile, Fey was not resting on the success of *30 Rock*. She spent much of the summer of 2007 shooting a new comedy movie. Fey did not write this one. Michael McCullers, who wrote two Austin Powers movie sequels, scripted it. But Fey was the star. Her costar was Amy Poehler. Actors in supporting roles included *Saturday Night Live* alumni Fred Armisen and Will Forte. The movie also featured established actors Steve Martin, Sigourney Weaver, and Greg Kinnear.

The movie was to be called *Baby Mama*. It would be released in 2008. Fey would play Kate Holbrook, an intelligent businesswoman with no boyfriend or husband. However, she wants to have a baby. She hires

Angie, played by Poehler, to be a surrogate mother, or a woman hired to have her baby. Kate then learns Angie is an immature and uneducated party girl. When Amy has no place to live, Kate takes her in. Kate accidentally gets trained for parenthood by having to take care of the babyish Amy. The opposites living together provides many laughs. But would *Baby Mama* be as big a hit as *Mean Girls?*

8

LABOR PAINS

s the second season of *30 Rock* began, Fey and the rest of the show's crew were looking foward to more episodes with bright comedy, sharp satire, and critical success. Then something happened that threw a monkey wrench in the works.

In the fall of 2007, television and other writers belonging to the Writers Guild of America (WGA), announced that its members were not being treated fairly. One major issue involved residuals. Writers are paid a salary for writing scripts for television programs. However, most hit television programs are later released on DVDs. DVD sales are a form of residuals. Since they wrote the scripts for those television shows, the writers felt they should be getting a fair portion of the money their employers, the Alliance of Motion Picture and Television Producers

(AMPTP), were making from DVD sales and rentals. In the fall of 2007, WGA members were getting only 0.3 percent to 0.36 percent of the cost of each DVD sold.[1] With DVD sales skyrocketing, the writers felt that portion was too low. However, the AMPTP said they could not afford to pay writers more for residuals. The AMPTP maintained they needed the extra money because costs to produce and promote their television programs had risen.

The writers also noticed that more and more viewers were watching television programs over the Internet. They wanted a fair portion of the money earned from that medium as well.

The writers seemed to have a point. Movie producers were making a lot more money from DVD rentals and purchases than showings in movie theaters. As late as 2004, Americans spent $1.78 billion dollars going to see movies in theaters. But at the same time, they spent $4.8 billion to buy and rent DVDs, a difference of more than $3 billion.[2]

On November 5, 2007, the WGA went on strike. The majority of actors supported the writers. Several took a public stance and walked the picket line, or the official protest gathering, of the striking writers. Tina Fey was one of those showing public support for the writers. As soon as the strike began, Fey was outside 30 Rockefeller Plaza, holding a picket sign and protesting with the writers.

She said, "I'm a member of the guild and I am here to support fellow guild members. This strike affects the show in which I work. We put our pens down yesterday, and we will not write until negotiations resume."[3] However, Fey continued to do jobs that did not involve writing, such as acting and producing. But she could only do so with scripts that had been turned in before the strike. Without writers turning in more scripts, there was soon nothing to produce or act in. On November 9, production of *30 Rock* was stopped.

Alec Baldwin wrote at the time: "*30 Rock* has had the kind of reception that writers can only dream of,

Tina Fey pickets with other members of the Writers Guild of America in front of Rockefeller Center on November 5, 2007, to show her support.

and I feel that all of our writers, and especially Tina, deserve everything that has come their way."[4]

The strike continued through the winter. Instead of seeing new episodes of their favorite shows, television viewers watched reruns. Since many had seen the reruns already, some stopped watching television altogether. They switched to reality television shows, which do not require written scripts. Despite the fact that they were missing the latest episodes of their favorite programs, the

Jerry Seinfeld, Tina Fey, and Alec Baldwin on the "Seinfeldvision" episode of *30 Rock*, which aired October 4, 2007.

majority of television viewers supported the writers. In one poll, 60 percent of the viewers said they sided with the writers. Just 14 percent supported the AMPTP.[5] The rest had no opinion.

In early February, the WGA and the AMPTP came to an agreement. It was voted on and approved on February 12, 2008. The WGA did not get all they wanted, but they did agree to a three-year deal including a higher percentage payment for residuals.

The members of the WGA went to work right away, but there was no way they could salvage an entire season—usually twenty-one or twenty-two episodes per series. For the 2007–2008 television season, *30 Rock* broadcast a total of fifteen episodes. The first *30 Rock* episode after the strike was aired on April 10, 2008.

Fey wrote or cowrote four of the fifteen episodes. In one, she makes fun of the low ratings' problems of her real-life network, NBC. Jack decides to digitally insert comedian Jerry Seinfeld into every show on NBC to get higher ratings. Seinfeld's own situation comedy, *Seinfeld,* aired on NBC in the 1990s and was one of the network's biggest all-time successes. In a different episode, Fey cowrote with writer Kay Cannon that Republican Jack falls in love with a Democratic congresswoman named C. C. Cunningham. C. C. appeared in three other episodes that season.

Fey poses with three of the seven Emmys *30 Rock* won on September 21, 2008: outstanding lead actress in a comedy series, outstanding writing in a comedy series, and outstanding comedy series.

While the television season was just resuming, *Baby Mama* was released on April 25, 2008. It was not as successful as *Mean Girls*, but it was a hit. Movie reviewers gave much of the credit to Fey and Poehler.

Critic Jim Lane of the *Sacramento News and Review* wrote: "Writer-director Michael McCullers' script is short on surprises, but it (is . . .) gracefully satisfying, and laughs are frequent. Best of all, McCullers knows a good thing when he has it, and he has Fey and Poehler, longtime pals (and *SNL* "Weekend Update" partners) who work together with easy joined-at-the-hip rapport; they could, with luck, be one of the great comedy teams."[6] M. B. Scott, who reviews movies for the newspaper the *New Orleans Times-Picayune,* wrote: "The two funny ladies are an appealing pair, with Fey's wry, deadpan delivery a perfect complement to Poehler's fearlessly juvenile brand of humor."[7]

Not all critics were as kind. Michael Phillips of the *Chicago Tribune* did not like the movie but said Fey and Poehler were not the problem. He blamed scriptwriter McCullers. Phillips wrote: "Midway through, though, I started wondering why I wasn't laughing more. *Baby Mama* was not written by Fey and/or Poehler, which may be the reason."[8] Some did not like it at all. Dana Stevens of the Web site *slate.com* called it "the most disappointing movie of the year so far."[9] But *Baby Mama* still made a profit. It cost $30 million to make and earned more than $64 million dollars.[10]

For the second straight year, *30 Rock* was one of the most honored television programs at the Emmy Awards. The show received seven, including outstanding comedy series. Fey personally won two Emmys—one for outstanding writing for a comedy series and the other for outstanding lead actress in a comedy series.[11]

9

"I CAN SEE RUSSIA FROM MY HOUSE!"

Something far from the television entertainment world was about to change Fey's life. The year 2008 was a presidential election year, and the Democratic nominee for president was Barack Obama, a senator from Illinois. Obama chose well-known Senator Joe Biden of Delaware as his running mate for vice president.

The Republican nominee for president was Arizona senator John McCain. There were a number of established Republicans McCain could have chosen as his running mate. Instead, McCain surprised nearly everyone by choosing someone very obscure: Governor Sarah Palin of Alaska.

While people were getting to know more about Governor Palin, they noticed something interesting.

With her dark hair and glasses, Palin bears a strong resemblance to Tina Fey. If Fey was still on *Saturday Night Live*, she would have been a natural choice to play Palin in satirical sketches. At first, Fey was not convinced about the resemblance. Then her husband said to her, "You really have to admit, you do look like her."[1] Fey admitted, "Well, I kinda do look like her. I'd better really listen to how this lady talks."[2]

Sure enough, Lorne Michaels asked Fey back to make a special guest appearance on *Saturday Night Live* as Palin. Fey spent the next few weeks practicing Palin's voice and mannerisms. Palin has a folksy manner. She would wink after making certain comments and use phrases such as "You betcha."

On September 11, 2008, Palin did a one-on-one interview with news anchor Charles Gibson. One question Gibson asked was Palin's opinion of the Bush Doctrine. The Bush Doctrine is the principle that the United States is justified in attacking in advance any nation viewed as a threat. Palin stumbled in answering the question, causing people to believe she did not know the meaning of the Bush Doctrine. Defenders of Palin said that many Americans did not understand the Bush Doctrine. Critics said that might be true, but a person running for vice president should understand it.

Palin had also been challenged about her lack of experience in foreign policy. As a governor, she dealt with matters concerning Alaska, but not other nations.

Those who liked Palin said in response that presidents Carter, Reagan, Clinton, and George W. Bush had served only as governors.

Palin stated that Alaska sits across the Bering Strait from Russia. She said that gave her expertise in foreign policy. In response, critics mocked her. They said that the parts of Russia and Alaska that sit near each other are sparsely inhabited wilderness. They added that Moscow, the capital of Russia, sits more than four thousand miles from Anchorage, the most populous city in Alaska.

Saturday Night Live premiered for the 2008–2009 season on September 13. The opening sketch paired Fey and Amy Poehler. Fey, of course, played Sarah Palin. Poehler played Hillary Clinton. Former First Lady Clinton had been a candidate for the Democratic nomination as president. In the sketch, Palin and Clinton said they were putting aside their differences to discuss the problem of sexism. Poehler portrayed Clinton as intelligent, but unfeminine and bossy. Fey portrayed Palin as attractive, but airheaded and ditsy.

When Poehler, as Hillary Clinton, said, "I believe that diplomacy is the cornerstone of any foreign policy," Fey, as Sarah Palin, flashed a big smile and responded, "And I can see Russia from my house." When Poehler affirmed, "I don't agree with the Bush Doctrine," Fey laughed embarrassingly and said shyly, "I don't know what that is."[3]

Tina Fey as Governor Sarah Palin and Amy Poehler as Senator Hillary Clinton on the September 13, 2008 episode of *Saturday Night Live*.

People had been looking forward to seeing Fey as Palin. That episode was the highest-rated episode of *Saturday Night Live* since the first episode after the terrorist attacks of September 11, 2001.[4]

Critics loved both women's performances. Erin Fox of *TV Guide* wrote: "How awesomely perfect is Tina Fey as Palin? Thank goodness they coaxed her back! She nails Palin's mannerisms and accent. Poehler is amazing as Hillary; her timing is better than ever. My favorite line was Tina saying 'I can see Russia from my house!'"[5]

The real Sarah Palin showed she has a sense of humor. Her spokesperson, Tracey Schmitt, laughed. "She [Palin] thought it was quite funny, particularly because she once dressed up as Tina Fey for Halloween."[6] It seemed that the only person who did not laugh at the sketch was John McCain's spokesperson, Carly Fiorina. According to Fiorina, the sketch about sexism was itself sexist. She said that it was "disrespectful in the extreme, and yes, I would say, sexist in the sense that just because Sarah Palin has different views than Hillary Clinton does not mean that she lacks substance. She has a lot of substance."[7]

Tina Fey appeared several more times in character as Sarah Palin on *SNL*. On September 27, Fey appeared as Palin while Amy Poehler played news anchor Katie Couric. The real Couric had interviewed Sarah Palin a few days earlier on CBS news. In that interview,

Palin seemed unsure of herself. She gave rambling and garbled answers to some questions. In the *SNL* sketch, Fey answered a question from Poehler that was almost a word-for-word copy of Palin's real answer to Couric.

The real Palin got some revenge when she appeared as herself on the October 18 episode of *SNL*. Liberal actor and Fey's *30 Rock* costar, Alec Baldwin, was the guest host.

In the opening sketch, Fey is in character as Palin at a fake press conference. The camera then cuts to a shot of the real Sarah Palin and Lorne Michaels backstage watching Fey. Baldwin approaches Michaels and mistakes the real Sarah Palin as Tina Fey.

After realizing that he is talking to the real Sarah Palin, Baldwin goes out to Fey and whispers in her ear. She reponds: "What? The real one? Byeee!" Fey quickly exits as Palin enters to proclaim "Live from New York, it's Saturday Night!!!"[8] Most observers felt that Palin was a good sport.

Although Fey's performances as Sarah Palin were just for entertainment, some in the media said the sketches had a negative effect on Palin's actual candidacy. At first Palin had high public approval ratings. As the campaign progressed, however, her approval ratings dropped. *Time* magazine wrote: "When voters close their eyes now and envision Public Palin, likely as not they see Tina Fey. It's impossible to say whether *SNL* drove the drop in Palin's approval or simply followed it. . . . After all, Real Palin really sat down with Real Couric and gave a Really Bad Interview. That counts for something, right?"[9]

Fey's Palin act even made news overseas. The British Broadcasting Company (BBC), based in London, also asked whether Fey's satire of Palin or the real Palin herself was hurting her approval ratings. The BBC wrote: "Some commentators go as far as to dub the 'Tina Fey Factor' one of the biggest challenges the Republican Vice-Presidential candidate faces."[10] The article reported that a poll of 314 Democrats, Republicans, and Independents viewed Palin in a negative light after watching the *Saturday Night Live* sketches.[11] On the other hand, the article quoted political analyst Professor Larry Sabato saying the skits had no effect on how the public saw Palin. Sabato said, "It's interesting, it's fun, but it has nothing to do with how people are voting."[12]

Fey never apologized for her portrayal of Palin. After all, *Saturday Night Live* has poked fun at politicians of all parties for years. Fey added, "I stand by the pieces as both fair and quite gentle."[13]

In the meantime, Fey's *SNL* guest appearances were credited with helping the show's ratings jump 70 percent over those of the previous season.[14]

Obama and Biden beat McCain and Palin in a landslide. Experts said the poor economy and the lingering war in Iraq were the main reasons for Obama's win. After the campaign ended, Fey said she would no longer be doing the Palin satire. She said, "I have to retire [doing Palin] just because I have to do my day job," working on *30 Rock*.[15] Fey's fame as the Palin impersonator may have indirectly helped *30 Rock*. When *30 Rock* premiered for the 2008-2009 season on October 30, its ratings were up 20 percent over the previous season.[16]

It was little surprise that between her regular work on *30 Rock*, her successful movie *Baby Mama*, and her guest appearances on *SNL* as Sarah Palin, Tina Fey received a major honor at year's end: "Entertainer of the Year" by the Associated Press (AP). The AP is a group of newspaper editors and writers. One voter, entertainment editor of the *Pittsburgh Post-Gazette* Sharon Eberson, said, "Tina Fey is such an obvious choice. She gave us funny when we really needed it and, in a year when women in politics were making huge strides, Fey stood out in the world of entertainment."[17]

Meanwhile, Fey and the staff of *30 Rock* rolled on in their third season. In the first episode, Liz considers adopting a baby. That idea does not work, but later on in the season she has a few boyfriends, but—of course—she succeeds with none. The season ended with a parody of the movie *Mamma Mia*, in which Jack tries to find his real father.

30 Rock's overall ratings still fall into the average category. Yet it still ranks highly with viewers in households that earn over $100,000 a year.[18] That makes it very good for advertisers. In addition, *30 Rock* received twenty-two nominations for Emmy awards for the 2008-2009 season.[19] Fey did not win best actress in a series that year. But she did win an Emmy for a guest appearance as Sarah Palin on *Saturday Night Live.* As she accepted the award, she stood next to Justin Timberlake, who won a similar honor. Fey gave special thanks to her producer. "I just want to say I wouldn't be here tonight if it wasn't for Lorne Michaels. Justin would still be very famous and very rich. But I would not be here."[20]

Once again, *30 Rock* won the Emmy for outstanding comedy series. As Fey accepted the award, she humorously said, "We want to thank everyone in

The real Sarah Palin laughs as she and Lorne Michaels watch Tina Fey portray her on the October 18, 2008 episode of *SNL*.

our crew in Long Island City, every person who works on the show, including Scotty at the front desk who always says, 'Have a nice weekend.' Every day of the week he says, 'Have a nice weekend.'"[21] The audience responded in laughter.

In addition to entertaining millions, Fey has made differences in people's personal lives. Her costar Tracy Morgan was arrested for suspicion of drunk driving in 2005 and 2006. He says he stopped drinking in part because of a discussion he had with Fey. Morgan admitted, "She told me to fly right. Tina Fey is down like four flat tires. I love her . . . That's my sister from another mother with a different color."[22]

When not busy with her jobs in television and as a parent, Fey does her share of charity work. She appeared with numerous other entertainers in a benefit performance titled "Night of Too Many Stars: An Overbooked Concert for Autism Education." The event raises money for schools and outreach programs for autistic children. In 2009, she received an award called "Mothers Who Make a Difference."[23] It is given by another charity Fey is active in: Love Our Children USA. This group works to prevent violence against children.

Charity work aside, Fey keeps busy as an entertainer. *30 Rock* still occupies most of her waking hours. However, she did find time to film a romantic comedy titled *Date Night* with Steve Carell, star of the television hit *The Office*. It was released on April 9, 2010.

Fey and Carell play a bored, married couple looking for excitement in their lives. They decide to go out for a night on the town and accidentally get involved with a crime they had nothing to do with. Most critics liked *Date Night* but were not wild about it. *New York Post* critic Lou Lumenick's opinion was typical, calling *Date Night* "a reasonably amusing way to pass Saturday night with a significant other."[24] And it did make a profit. Fey also did the voice of a main character in the superhero comedy *Megamind*, released on November 7.

Just two days later, Fey received an honor of a lifetime. The Kennedy Center, a famous performing arts center in Washington, D.C., annually gives out a special award: the Mark Twain Prize for American Humor. Past honorees include Whoopi Goldberg, Bob Newhart, Steve Martin, and Bill Cosby. Fey was the 2010 award winner.

At age forty, she is the youngest person so far to win the Twain Prize. Comedy actor Betty White, eighty-eight years old, referred to Fey's youth in a speech at the award ceremony. White said, "She's so young. I just hope I can hang on long enough to see what she accomplishes when she learns to drive."[25]

During the event, Fey's friends and costars both kidded and praised her. Steve Martin said, "Isn't it refreshing to find a female comedian who's both really good and funny looking. Excuse me, that should have read, 'really funny and good looking.'"[26]

Tina Fey arrives at the Kennedy Center in Washington, D.C., to receive the Mark Twain Prize for American Humor, November 9, 2010.

Fellow *SNL* star Seth Meyers commended her: "I learned more about being a comedy writer from Tina Fey than anyone else. And the thing that I'll always remember about her is that she always had her sketch in her hand, all week long. It was a reminder to the rest of us that you could always be making your work better, always looking for one more joke."[27]

Fey was the last one to speak. After cracking some jokes, she said, "I'm so proud to represent American humor. I'm proud to be American."[28] She concluded, "And I'm most proud that even during trying times . . . we as a nation retain our sense of humor."[29]

CHRONOLOGY

1970   Elizabeth Stamatina Fey born May 18 in Upper Darby, Pennsylvania.

ca. 1975   Attacked in front yard, results in permanent scar on her face.

mid-1980s   Writes satirical column under a pseudonym for high-school newspaper.

1988   Graduates high school.

1988–1992   Attends University of Virginia; directs plays for young people during summers.

1992   Moves to Chicago to study improvisational comedy at Second City; takes classes for nine months.

1993   Acts with Second City's touring company; starts dating director/writer Jeff Richmond.

1994–1997   Performs at Second City's home theater in Chicago.

1997   Hired as a writer for *Saturday Night Live.*

1999   Named *Saturday Night Live*'s head writer.

1999–2000   Performs improvisational show "Dratch and Fey" with Rachel Dratch.

2000   Becomes coanchor of *Saturday Night Live*'s "Weekend Update" segment with cast member Jimmy Fallon.

2001	Marries Jeff Richmond on June 3; nominated for but does not win first Emmy award for outstanding writing of a variety, music, or comedy program; wins writing award from Writers Guild of America.
2002	Wins first Emmy award for outstanding writing for a variety, music, or comedy program, *Saturday Night Live.*
2004	*Mean Girls* is released to theaters on April 30.
2006	Leaves *Saturday Night Live* in May; *30 Rock* debuts on October 11.
2007	*30 Rock* wins Emmy award for outstanding comedy series; takes part in Writers Guild of America strike that begins on November 5.
2008	Writers Guild of America strike settled on February 12; first new episode of *30 Rock* after strike is aired on April 10; movie *Baby Mama* is released in theaters on April 25; Fey wins two personal Emmy awards for *30 Rock*; *30 Rock* wins Emmy for outstanding comedy series; first plays Sarah Palin as guest star on *Saturday Night Live* on September 13.
2009	*30 Rock* nominated for twenty-two Emmy awards, wins outstanding comedy series; Fey wins Emmy for guest appearance as Sarah Palin on *Saturday Night Live.*
2010	*Date Night* released April 9; *Megamind* released November 7; receives the Mark Twain Prize for American Humor on November 9.

CHAPTER NOTES

Chapter 1. *30 Rock* Rocks!

1. Kristen Baldwin, "One Fine Fey," *Entertainment Weekly,* April 13, 2007, <http://www.ebscohost.com/> (June 10, 2009).

2. Tad Friend, "Shows About Shows," *New Yorker,* April 24, 2006, <http://www.newyorker.com/archive/2006/04/24/060424ta_talk_friend> (June 10, 2009).

3. Ibid.

4. Marc D. Allen, "Polished 'Rock' Rolls On," *Washington Post,* August 26, 2007, <http://www.washingtonpost.com/wp-dyn/content/article/2007/08/22/AR2007082201741_pf.html> (August 26, 2009).

5. Kevin Chong, "Ain't It Funny," *Canadian Broadcasting Company,* December 11, 2007, <http://www.cbc.ca/arts/tv/fey.html> (August 27, 2009).

Chapter 2. Sitting With the Brainiac Nerds

1. Joe Barbera, *My Life in Toons* (Atlanta, Ga.: Turner Publishing, Inc., 1994), p. 141.

2. Ibid., p. 136.

3. Tim Brooks and Earle Marsh, *The Complete Directory to Prime Time Network and Cable TV Shows* (New York: Ballantine Books, 2007), p. 1682.

4. Ibid., p. 1683.

5. Noel Murray, "Tina Fey," *A.V. Club,* November 1, 2006, <http://www.avclub.com/articles/tina-fey,14025/> (June 10, 2009).

6. Heidi Mitchell, "Tina's Way," *Town and Country,* February 2009, <http://www.ebscohost.com/> (June 10, 2009).

7. Maureen Dowd, "What Tina Wants," *Vanity Fair,* January 2009, p. 72.

8. Ibid.

9. Murray.

10. Ibid.

11. Oprah Winfrey, "Oprah Talks to Tina Fey," *O, The Oprah Magazine,* February 2009, <http://www.oprah.com/article/omagazine/200902_omag_ocut_tina_fey/2> (July 31, 2009).

12. Eric Spitznagel, "Tina Fey," *Believer,* November 2003, <http://www.believermag.com/issues/200311/?read=interview_fey> (August 16, 2010).

13. Ibid.

14. Donna Freydkin, "Fey Gets Her Skewers Out," *USA Today,* April 23, 2004, <http://www.ebscohost.com/> (June 11, 2009).

15. Stephen Armstrong, "Tina Fey and the Success of *30 Rock*," *Times Online,* February 22, 2009, <http://entertainment.timesonline. co.uk/tol/arts_and_entertainment/tv_and_radio/article5766865.ece> (August 11, 2009).

16. Personal interview with Harry Dietzler, September 21, 2009.

17. "Tina Fey Gets the Last Laugh," *FoxNews.com,* April 25, 2004, <http://www.foxnews.com/story/0,2933,118079,00.html> (June 10, 2009).

18. Ibid.

19. Ibid.

20. Ibid.

21. George Everit, "Tina Fey," *SuicideGirls.com,* May 10, 2004, <http://suicidegirls.com/interviews/Tina+Fey/> (June 20, 2009).

Chapter 3. First Rate at Second City

1. Maureen Dowd, "What Tina Wants," *Vanity Fair,* January 2009, p. 69.

2. Kelly Tracy, "Funny Girl," *CosmoGirl,* February 2008, <http://www.cosmogirl.com/lifeadvice/project-2024/tina-fey-feb08> (July 21, 2009).

3. Christopher Goodwin, "And Funny With It," *Guardian,* May 11, 2008, <http://www.guardian.co.uk/lifeandstyle/2008/ may/11/women.television> (August 26, 2009).

4. Heidi Mitchell, "Tina's Way," *Town and Country,* February 2009, <http://www.ebscohost.com/> (June 10, 2009).

5. Jason Gay, "Meet Four-Eyed New Sex Symbol, 'Weekend Update' Anchor Tina Fey," *New York Observer,* March 4, 2001, <http://www.observer.com/node/44088> (August 4, 2009).

6. Personal interview with Harry Dietzler, September 21, 2009.

7. Ibid.

8. Personal interview with Stacy Moscotti Smith, September 23, 2009

9. Ibid.

10. Personal interview with Harry Dietzler, September 21, 2009.

11. Personal interview with Stacy Moscotti Smith, September 23, 2009.

12. Noel Murray, "Tina Fey," *A.V. Club,* November 1, 2006, <http://www.avclub.com/articles/tina-fey,14025/> (June 10, 2009).

13. Tracy.

14. Eric Spitznagel, "Tina Fey" *Believer,* November 2003, <http://www.believermag.com/issues/200311/?read=interview_fey> (August 16, 2010).

15. Ibid.

16. Ibid.

17. "Tina Fey Biography," *Notable Biographies,* n.d., <http://www.notablebiographies.com/news/Ca-Ge/Fey-Tina.html> (June 10, 2009).

18. Dowd, p. 72.

19. Ibid., p. 121.

20. Ibid., p. 72.

21. Ibid.

22. Kyle Smith and Brenda Rodriguez, "Leap of Fey," *People,* May 3, 2004, <http://www.ebscohost.com/> (June 11, 2009).

23. Excerpt of "Second City: First Family of Comedy," *YouTube,* August 18, 2008, <http://www.youtube.com/watch?v=tIvOUoYZhoU> (July 27, 2009).

24. Ibid.

25. Murray

26. Excerpt of "Second City: First Family of Comedy," *YouTube,* August 18, 2008, <http://www.youtube.com/watch?v=IDaWkAL-1lM&NR=1> (July 27, 2009).

27. Ibid.

28. Ibid.

....

Chapter 4. Long Days at *Saturday Night Live*

1. Jancee Dunn, "Funny Girl," *Reader's Digest,* April 2008, pp. 94–95.

2. Transcript of *Charlie Rose Show,* originally broadcast

on PBS, April 27, 2004, <http://www.charlierose.com/guest/view/1518> (July 22, 2009).

3. Excerpt of "Second City: First Family of Comedy," *YouTube,* August 18, 2008, <http://www.youtube.com/watch?v=tIvOUoYZhoU> (July 27, 2009).

4. Excerpt of "Second City: First Family of Comedy," *YouTube,* August 18, 2008, <http://www.youtube.com/watch?v=IDaWkAL-1lM&NR=1> <July 27, 2009>.

5. Eric Spitznagel, "Tina Fey" *Believer,* November 2003, <http://www.believermag.com/issues/200311/?read=interview_fey> (August 16, 2010).

6. Donna Freydkin, "Fey Gets Her Skewers Out," *USA Today,* April 23, 2004, <http://www.ebscohost.com/> (June 11, 2009).

7. Tim Townsend, "Comic Duo Splits Sides," *Wall Street Journal,* July 7, 2000, <http://online.wsj.com/article/SB962934366661558768.html?mod=googlewsj> (July 31, 2009).

8. Ibid.

9. Ibid.

10. Tom Shales and James Andrew Miller, *Live From New York* (Boston: Little, Brown and Company, 2002), p. 440.

11. Ibid., p. 441.

12. Ibid.

13. Dennis Miller and Rebecca Winters, "10 Questions for Dennis Miller," *CNN.com,* December 15, 2003, <http://www.cnn.com/2003/ALLPOLITICS/12/15/timep.miller.tm/> (August 3, 2009).

Chapter 5. "Dream Jobs to People—But They Are Also Very Hard"

1. Heidi Mitchell, "Tina's Way," *Town and Country,* February 2009, <http://www.ebscohost.com/> (June 10, 2009).

2. Jason Gay, "Meet Four-Eyed New Sex Symbol, 'Weekend Update' Anchor Tina Fey," *New York Observer,* March 4, 2001, <http://www.observer.com/node/44088> (August 4, 2009)

3. Eric Spitznagel, "Tina Fey" *Believer,* November 2003, <http://www.believermag.com/issues/200311/?read=interview_fey> (August 16, 2010).

4. Jancee Dunn, "Funny Girl," *Reader's Digest,* April 2008, p. 95.

5. Gay.

6. Ibid.

7. Kyle Smith and Brenda Rodriguez, "Leap of Fey," *People,* May 3, 2004, <http://www.ebscohost.com/> (June 11, 2009).

8. Virginia Heffernan, "Anchor Woman," *New Yorker,* November 3, 2003, <http://www.newyorker.com/archive/2003/11/03/031103fa_fact> (August 10, 2009).

9. Missy Schwartz, "The Smartest Girl in the Class," *Entertainment Weekly,* May 7, 2004, <http://www.ebscohost.com/> (June 10, 2009).

10. Transcript of *Charlie Rose Show,* originally broadcast on PBS, April 27, 2004, <http://www.charlierose.com/guest/view/1518> (July 22, 2009.)

11. "Tina Fey Gets the Last Laugh," *FoxNews.com,* April 25, 2004, <http://www.foxnews.com/story/0,2933,118079,00.html> (June 10, 2009).

12. Schwartz.

13. "Tina Fey Biography," *Notable Biographies,* n.d., <http://www.notablebiographies.com/news/Ca-Ge/Fey-Tina.html>.

14. Transcript of *Charlie Rose Show.*

15. Donna Freydkin, "Fey Gets Her Skewers Out," *USA Today,* April 23, 2004, <http://www.ebscohost.com/> (June 11, 2009).

16. Transcript of *Charlie Rose Show.*

17. Ibid.

Chapter 6. The Making of a Landmark Movie

1. Personal interview with Harry Dietzler, September 21, 2009.

2. Missy Schwartz, "The Smartest Girl in the Class," *Entertainment Weekly,* May 7, 2004, <http://www.ebscohost.com/> (June 10, 2009).

3. "Tina Fey Biography," *Notable Biographies,* n.d., <http://www.notablebiographies.com/news/Ca-Ge/Fey-Tina.html> (June 10, 2009).

4. Associated Press, "Tina Fey: Bookish Bombshell," *MSNBC.com,* May 4, 2004, <http://www.msnbc.msn.com/id/4854468/print/1/displaymode/1098/> (July 30, 2009).

5. Joel Stein, "Goddess of the Geeks," *Time* (South Pacific), June 21, 2004, <http://www.ebscohost.com/> (June 10, 2009).

6. "Amy Poehler," *The Internet Movie Database,* 2010, <http://www.imdb.com/name/nm0688132/> (August 19, 2009); "Rachel McAdams," *The Internet Movie Database,* 2010, <http://www.imdb.com/name/nm1046097/> (August 19, 2009).

7. Transcript of *Charlie Rose Show,* originally broadcast on PBS, April 27, 2004, <http://www.charlierose.com/guest/view/1518> (July 22, 2009).

8. Schwartz.

9. "Mean Girls," *Box Office Mojo,* n.d., <http://www.boxoffic-emojo.com/movies/?id=meangirls.htm> (August 19, 2009).

10. Brandon Gay, "'Mean Girls' Surprisingly Nice $24.4M Weekend," *Box Office Mojo,* May 3, 2004, <http://www.boxoffic-emojo.com/news/?id=1325&p=.htm> (August 19, 2009).

11. Ibid.

12. Ibid.

13. Ibid.

14. Ann Hornaday, "Comedy That Cliques," *Washington Post,* April 30, 2004, <http://www.washingtonpost.com/wp-dyn/content/article/2004/04/30/AR2005033113114.html> (August 20, 2009).

15. Moira McDonald, "'Mean Girls' Follows Catty Cliques Who Roam High School Hallways," *Seattle Times,* April 30, 2004, <http://community.seattletimes.nwsource.com/archive/?slug=mean30&date=20040430> (August 20, 2009).

16. Nev Pierce, "Mean Girls (2004)," *British Broadcasting Company,* June 17, 2004, <http://www.bbc.co.uk/wiltshire/entertainment/films_and_tv/mean_girls.shtml> (June 24, 2009).

17. Rosalind Wiseman, "'Queen Bee Moms and Kingpin Dads,'" *Washington Post,* March 29, 2006, <http://www.washingtonpost.com/wp-dyn/content/discussion/2006/03/23/DI2006032300970_pf.html> (August 10, 2009).

18. "Mean Girls," *Box Office Mojo.*

Chapter 7. Liz and Jack in the Television World

1. Tad Friend, "Shows About Shows," *New Yorker,* April 24, 2006, <http://www.newyorker.com/archive/2006/04/24/060424ta_talk_friend> (June 10, 2009).

2. Alec Baldwin, "Tina Fey," *Interview,* April 2004, <http://www.ebscohost.com/> (June 10, 2009).

3. Donna Freydkin, "Amy Poehler Updates Her 'SNL' Career," *USA Today,* November 25, 2004, <http://www.usatoday.com/life/people/2004-11-25-poehler-SNL_x.htm> (August 27, 2009).

4. Donna Freydkin, "It's News to Them: Co-anchors Make 'SNL' History," *USA Today,* November 25, 2004, <http://www.usatoday.com/life/television/news/2004-11-25-SNL-update_x.htm> (August 27, 2009).

5. Ibid.

6. Freydkin, "Amy Poehler Updates Her 'SNL' Career."

7. Ibid.

8. Gavin Edwards, "A Dangerous Woman," *Rolling Stone,* December 14, 2006, <http://www.ebscohost.com/> (June 10, 2009).

9. Kristen Baldwin, "One Fine Fey," *Entertainment Weekly,* April 13, 2007, <http://www.ebscohost.com/> (June 10, 2009).

10. Emma Rosenbaum, "Rachel Rolls With It," *New York Magazine,* October 16, 2006, <http://nymag.com/news/intelligencer/22836/> (August 28, 2009).

11. Cassidy Hartmann, "A Simple Twist of Fey," *Philadelphia Weekly,* October 11, 2006, <http://www.philadelphiaweekly.com/news-and-opinion/cover-story/a_simple_twist_of_fey-38419914.html> (July 31, 2009).

12. Baldwin.

13. Ibid.

14. James Poniewozik, "Do Not Adjust Your Set," *Time,* September 18, 2006, <http://www.time.com/time/magazine/article/0,9171,1535853,00.html> (August 27, 2009).

15. Roger Friedman, "'Studio 60' Cancellation Imminent," *Fox News,* November 3, 2006, <http://www.foxnews.com/story/0,2933,226092,00.html> (September 3, 2009).

16. Ibid.

17. Ibid.

18. Marc D. Allen, "Polished 'Rock' Rolls On," *Washington Post,* August 26, 2007, <http://www.washingtonpost.com/wp-dyn/content/article/2007/08/22/AR2007082201741_pf.html> (August 26, 2009).

19. Ibid.

20. Ibid.

21. Ibid.

22. Associated Press, "'30 Rock' Renewed by Optimistic NBC," *MSNBC,* April 8, 2007, <http://www.msnbc.msn.com/id/17955445/> (August 26, 2009).

Chapter 8. Labor Pains

1. "WGA Contract 2007 Proposals," *Writers Guild of America,* n.d., <http://www.wga.org/subpage_member.aspx?id=2485> (September 8, 2009).

2. Sharon Waxman, "Studios Rush to Cash in On DVD Boom; Swelling Demand for Disks Alters Hollywood's Arithmetic," *New York Times,* April 20, 2004, <http://www.nytimes.com/2004/04/20/movies/studios-rush-cash-dvd-boom-swelling-demand-for-disks-alters-hollywood-s.html> (September 8, 2009).

3. Steve Gorman, "Hollywood Writers Start Strike After Talks Collapse," *Reuters,* November 5, 2007, <http://www.reuters.com/article/idUSN0522255420071105> (September 8, 2009).

4. Alec Baldwin, "What the Strike Is Costing us," *Huffington Post,* November 11, 2007, <http://www.huffingtonpost.com/alec-baldwin/what-the-strike-is-costin_b_72120.html> (September 8, 2009).

5. Gary Levin, "Poll: Viewers Side With Striking Writers," *USA Today,* December 19, 2007, <http://www.usatoday.com/life/television/news/2007-12-18-strike-poll_N.htm> (September 8, 2009).

6. Jim Lane, "Baby Mama," *Sacramento News and Review,* May 1, 2008, <http://www.newsreview.com/sacramento/content?oid=660204> (September 10, 2009).

7. M. B. Scott, "'Baby Mama' a Comedy That Delivers," *New Orleans Times-Picayune,* April 25, 2008, <http://www.nola.com/movies/index.ssf/2008/04/baby_mama_a_comedy_that_delive.html> (September 10, 2009).

8. Michael Phillips, "Movie Review: 'Baby Mama,'" *Chicago Tribune,* April 25, 2008, <http://chicago.metromix.com/movies/movie_review/movie-review-baby-mama/388170/content> (September 10, 2009).

9. Dana Stevens, "Womb Service," *Slate,* April 24, 2008, <http://www.slate.com/id/2189886/> (September 10, 2009).

10. "Baby Mama," *Box Office Mojo,* n.d., <http://www.boxoffic-emojo.com/movies/?id=babymama.htm> (September 10, 2009).

11. "Advanced Primetime Awards Search," *Academy of Television Arts and Sciences,* n.d., <http://www.emmys.org/awards/awardsearch.php> (September 10, 2009).

Chapter 9. "I Can See Russia From My House!"

1. Jennifer Armstrong, "No. 2 Tina Fey," *Entertainment Weekly,* November 21, 2008, <http://www.ebscohost.com/> (June 10, 2009).

2. Associated Press, "Tina Fey Is AP Entertainer of the Year," *Variety,* December 23, 2008, <http://www.variety.com/awardcentral_article/VR1117997736.html?na...> (December 24, 2008).

3. Excerpt of *Saturday Night Live* segment from *CelebTV.com, YouTube,* September 16, 2008, <http://www.youtube.com/watch?v=FdDqSvJ6aHc> (September 11, 2009).

4. Ibid.

5. Erin Fox, "TV Show Recaps: Michael Phelps Hosts, Lil Wayne Performs," *TV Guide,* September 14, 2008, <http://www.tvguide.com/episode-recaps/Saturday-Night-Live/Michael-Phelps-Hosts-17300.aspx> (September 11, 2009).

6. "Sarah Palin Reacts to Tina Fey Impersonation," *Entertainment Tonight,* September 15, 2008, <http://www.etonline.com/news/2008/09/65530/index.html> (September 11, 2009).

7. "Carly Fiorina Criticizes Tina Fey As 'Disrespectful . . . Sexist,'" *Huffington Post,* September 15, 2008, <http://www.huffingtonpost.com/2008/09/15/carly-fiorina-criticizes_n_126533.html> (September 11, 2009).

8. NBC Universal, Media Village press release, October 19, 2008, <http://nbcumv.com/entertainment/release_detail.nbc/entertainment-20081019000000-governorsarahpalin.html> (September 12, 2009).

9. James Poniewozik, "Palin vs. Palin," *Time,* October 20, 2008, <http://www.ebscohost.com/> (June 10, 2009).

10. Rajini Vaidyanathan, "Palin Mimic Gets US Public's Vote," *British Broadcasting Company News,* October 11, 2008, <http://newsvote.bbc.co.uk/mpapps/pagetools/print/news.bbc.co.uk/2/hi/americas/us_elections_2008/7665644.stm> (June 24, 2009).

11. Ibid.

12. Ibid.

13. "Palin's Mimic 'Glues Down Ears,'" *British Broadcasting Company News,* October 22, 2008, <http://newsvote.bbc.co.uk/mpapps/pagetools/print/news.bbc.co.uk/2/hi/entertainment/7683689.stm> (June 24, 2009).

14. Jennifer Armstrong, "Tina Fey Says She's Retiring Sarah Palin Impersonation," *Entertainment Weekly,* November 5, 2008, <http://hollywoodinsider.ew.com/2008/11/tina-fey-says-s.html?iid=top2> (June 11, 2009).

15. Ibid.

16. Ibid.

17. Associated Press.

18. "The Curious Case of 30 Rock," *TV by the Numbers,* April 4, 2009, <http://tvbythenumbers.com/2009/04/04/the-curious-case-of-30-rock/15925> (September 12, 2009).

19. 2009 nominations list, *Academy of Television Arts and Sciences,* <http://cdn.emmys.tv/awards/2009ptemmys/61stemmys_nomswin.php#1> (September 12, 2009).

20. *61st Primetime Emmy Awards* broadcast, September 20, 2009, CBS, Don Mischer executive producer.

21. Ibid.

22. Donna Freydkin, "Morgan Just Keeps Climbing," *USA Today,* July 23, 2009, p. 2D.

23. "Tina Fey's Charity Work," *Look to the Stars: The World of Celebrity Giving,* n.d., <http://www.looktothestars.org/celebrity/1731-tina-fey> (September 12, 2009).

24. Lou Lumenick, "Hard Dazed Night," *New York Post,* April 9, 2010, <http://www.nypost.com/p/entertainment/movies/hard_dazed_night_h1PqfasDu1hQmFcQCanrPP> (November 16, 2010).

25. Mark Krantz Productions, Comedia Inc., *The Thirteenth Annual Kennedy Center Mark Twain Prize: Celebrating Tina Fey,* aired on PBS November 14, 2010.

26. Ibid.

27. Ibid.

28. Ibid.

29. Ibid.

FURTHER READING

Belli, Mary Lou, and Dinah Lenney. *Acting for Young Actors: The Ultimate Teen Guide.* New York: Backstage Books, 2006.

Friedman, Lauri S. *Tina Fey.* Detroit: Gale Cengage, 2010.

Hubbard-Brown, Janet. *Tina Fey: Writer and Actress.* New York: Chelsea House Publications, 2010.

Madison, Patricia Ryan. *Improv Wisdom: Don't Prepare, Just Show Up.* New York: Harmony/Bell Tower, 2005.

McKnight, Katherine S., and Mary Scruggs. *The Second City Guide to Improvisation in the Classroom: Using Improvisation to Teach Skills and Boost Learning.* San Francisco, Calif.: Jossey-Bass, 2008.

INTERNET ADDRESSES

"Tina Fey," *TV.com*
http://www.tv.com/tina-fey/person/40079/summary.html

30 Rock Web site
http://www.nbc.com/30-rock/

The Second City Web site
http://www.secondcity.com/

INDEX